Introduction
The changing context

Alan Moys

Almost a decade ago I wrote a chapter for the CILT publication *Teaching languages to adults*[1] which was published in 1984. In September of the same year, CILT organised a national conference for teachers of languages to adults, with a particular focus on the need for professional support, adequate resources and proper recognition for a field which still often attracted Cinderella references even though it represented a major slice of the adult education cake. How much has changed? Perhaps, given the stresses under which adult education has so long operated, the question should be, *How much has changed for the better?* While it has become something of a cliché to speak of the rate of educational change in recent years, a review of developments as they concern the adult language learner in this country is an exercise which is revealing in its significance for the future in terms both of what happens in classrooms and how the learning of languages fits into a broader educational and social frame.

Perhaps the most remarkable - and one hopes the most enduring - change has happened outside classrooms. In the last few years we have witnessed in this country a major surge in the level of public awareness of the importance of competence in languages. Back in 1984, who could have foreseen that by the end of the decade the year 1992 would have taken on an even more apocalyptic symbolism than 1984 itself, for all its Orwellian connotations? Who could have dreamed that in 1990 the Department of Trade and Industry would launch an expensive publicity campaign with full page advertisements in the daily press and posters on street hoardings urging British business to do something about its language skills? Who would have forecast the crop of newspaper articles, television and radio broadcasts, and offers of language courses at all levels which have appeared in recent years? Who would have guessed that many teachers of languages would now be entering in their diaries each year a reminder to attend the London Language Show, another sign of the changing times?

Political and policy decisions have been at the heart of this most significant shift in public attitudes, and while it may be debatable just how lasting will be the effects, there are good reasons to believe that the dogged British refusal to learn other languages is fast becoming more of a

A broader educational framework

The National Curriculum

stereotype than an accurate reflection of reality. The Government's decision to include the learning of a foreign language as a foundation subject in the National Curriculum for all school pupils from 11-16 sends very important messages to learners, parents and teachers that this country cannot afford to have half its young people abandon the learning of other languages by the age of 14, which was the position until the National Curriculum legislation was produced. It is also Government policy that we should seek to diversify the range of languages on offer in our education system, though any significant reorientation at school level will require substantial funding in terms of linguistic retraining, given the traditional imbalance in favour of French.

The European context

But if policy developments at national level in recent years have reinforced and reflected changing public attitudes, it is the context of European Community policy which quite naturally lies at the heart of our new view about developing a national capability in languages. On the one hand the legislation leading to the Single European Market is providing a spur to British business to learn to operate in the language of its European customers and competitors. While the economic recession has severely restricted investment in new training just at the time when employers were becoming convinced of the critical relationship between language competence and business success, there is every sign that the business world in this country is now 'thinking European' on an increasing scale.

ERASMUS

We would be forgiven for thinking that European policy initiatives have been exclusively in the economic field, but in education also there have been European developments of great importance to the subject under discussion. In particular, Community schemes to promote exchanges and work experience among students and young employees have had a dramatic impact on the 16-25 age-group. An excellent illustration of this effect is provided by the ERASMUS[2] programme, a scheme under which students (and indeed teachers) in higher education spend a term in a university in another member state, as part of their degree programme. Such has been the success of this scheme that now every UK institution of higher education has at least one ERASMUS programme. The effect on students' attitudes to language learning has been remarkable. Throughout the country, universities, polytechnics and colleges have reported spectacular growth in demand for language courses from students in other disciplines, prompted in many cases by the immediate challenge of a period of study in another European country. Many higher education institutions have launched schemes to make language learning available (and in some cases obligatory) for all students. There are indications that this development is having also a backwash effect on students in the 16-19 age group in schools and colleges. Demand (and provision) here is increasing, but the 16-19 range still urgently awaits the sort of reform which will provide a broader and more balanced curriculum of the sort which will give appropriate weight to competence in languages.

LINGUA

In 1989 European education ministers gave their agreement to the EC LINGUA[3] programme, with funding available from 1990 for the purpose of achieving a qualitative and quantitative improvement in foreign language teaching and learning in the twelve member states. One of the less trumpeted effects of the 1992 Maastricht Treaty, if it survives its pre-ratification agonies, will be that school education will come within the competence of the European Community. For programmes such as LINGUA the Community has hitherto had to seek from member states specific agreements outside its legal competence or to restrict (however nominally) its involvement to the field of **training**, where its brief is covered by the Treaty of Rome. Thus it is that the LINGUA programme in its present pre-Maastricht form does not target school pupils below the age of 16. Nonetheless, it represents a substantial investment in our future linguistic capability, and provides valuable funding support for visits and exchanges of young people in vocational training, for the encouragement of language training in business, and for the in-service training of teachers. The UK is a major partner in the LINGUA programme, not least because of the demand for English from other countries. We can expect this programme to have a steadily increasing impact on language learning, not least in the adult education field.

New technology

Our growing internationalisation of outlook is of course not exclusively the result of political decisions on the European front. The rapid developments in recent years in the technology of television transmission mean that world events are beamed directly to us as they happen. The arrival and proliferation of the satellite as a means of programme delivery gives us (both private citizens and in our schools and colleges) the potential of immediate access to the daily television output of Brussels, Rome, Madrid and Moscow. The information technology revolution means that we can send and receive textual communications with correspondents in other countries for the price of - and at the speed of - a telephone call. The widespread availability in our homes of video recording and the increasing popularity of the small portable video camera represent a major resource both for the teacher of languages and for the learner - and particularly the adult learner who may wish or need to learn independently[4].

NVQs

So far we have been looking at those pressures, influences and opportunities which are having an increased motivational effect on language learners and particularly on adult learners. There have been in addition important developments in recent years which will impinge on the decisions that adult learners and their teachers take about what is to be learned and for what purpose. Notable among these has been the move by the Government to develop standardised national measures of competence across all vocational fields:

> *A National Vocational Qualification is defined as a statement of competence clearly relevant to work and intended to facilitate entry into, or progression in, employment, further education and training, issued by a recognised body to an individual.*
> (National Council for Vocational Qualifications[5]:
> *The NVQ criteria and related guidance, p 8)*

The system of NVQs and the standard which they represent are likely to have a decisive effect on foreign language courses as on all vocationally related programmes. At the time of writing, standards for languages are about to be published, and examining and awarding bodies will be aligning their examinations and qualifications to the NVQ requirements[6]. Employers, through the lead bodies for different occupations, will be incorporating the languages NVQs as components into occupational qualifications as diverse as travel and tourism on the one hand and sales and marketing on the other.

Funding issues
The implications of the NVQ development for teachers of languages to adults are wide-ranging. Let us briefly consider two very distinct but ultimately related effects. The whole system has been constructed around the model of **competence** as the basis for the elaboration of the standards. This means that qualifications - and therefore the courses we teach - will be defined in terms of learning **outcomes**, that is what a learner can **do** rather than what he or she may know. Fortunately, this is very much the direction which foreign language learning courses and targets have been taking over the recent years, and will not therefore come as a shock to most teachers. More worrying is the related pressure on the part of the Government to seek to discriminate for funding purposes in favour of vocational courses in the adult field at the expense of leisure courses. This arbitrary distinction is ultimately unsustainable, as is particularly evident in the language learning field, but it is likely to threaten the heterogeneity and richness of the adult language class as many of us have known it.

So much for the context, which promises to be both rewarding, and here and there difficult. Adult education tutors are no strangers to difficulty, but can look forward to enhanced professional - if not material - rewards in the context outlined in this introductory chapter. The rest of this book is devoted to the much more important discussion of ways and means. It provides a rich seam of expertise and experience on the part of the editors and contributors.

Alan Moys
former Director of CILT

References

1. Sidwell, D (ed), *Teaching languages to adults*, CILT (1984).

2. ERASMUS
   Information about the EC ERASMUS programme is obtainable from the UK Students' Grant Council, The University Research and Development Building, Canterbury CT2 7PD. Tel: 0227 762712.

3. LINGUA
   Information and a regular newsletter are obtainable from the UK Lingua Unit, Seymour Mews House, Seymour Mews, London W1H 9PE. Tel: 071 224 1477.

4. *Technology in Language Learning*
   Series of six titles published by CILT, details on demand.

5. National Council for Vocational Qualifications (NCVQ)
   222 Euston Road, London NW1 2BZ. Tel: 071 387 9898.

6. The agency equivalent to NCVQ in Scotland is SCOTVEC, Hanover House, 24 Douglas Street, Glasgow G2 7NQ. Tel: 041 248 7900.

The adult language learner   1

Learning as an adult

Duncan Sidwell

The first three units of this publication deal with the adult language learner's motivations and needs. These are, of course, to be satisfied within the context of how adult education is provided, and it may be worthwhile to look first at the direction which the provision of adult education appears to be taking at the end of this century. In general, adult education is becoming more market-orientated and vocational in its emphasis. Consideration and funding are being given to the provision of courses which lead to job-related or other examination qualifications, while courses defined as 'for leisure interests'[1] will be more likely to have to be self-sustaining and rely upon discretionary support. There is also, as far as language learning is concerned, a considerable increase in interest and recognition of its value. The introduction of language learning by the Open University and the Open College system is evidence of this. This growth in interest is also leading to more private provision. We can expect, therefore, a heightened customer awareness to accompany this increase in demand and a consequent need to respond with higher professional standards of provision.

This first unit presents some of the characteristics and concerns of adult students. It looks at motivation, expectations and age as three important factors in the education of adults.

Adult students as individuals

When people sign up to follow a course in adult education they do so with very varied motivations and from a variety of backgrounds. Previous experience, age, immediate wishes, needs and hopes for the future all play a part in the decision to join a language class. The objective of all the students may be the same - to learn to speak the target language, but the reasons why they have chosen to do so, the expectations they have of how the process will be carried out, and their individual feelings about their learning, will all differ widely. It is important, therefore, when we generalise about the adult student and, more importantly, when tutors first meet their classes, to bear in mind that the experience of going into a language class has a very different meaning for each student in it.

Motivation

The motivation which brings a person to join a group is usually quite complex, combining conscious and unconscious motives. We shall be looking at some aspects of unconscious motivation later, but will first look at some of the conscious purposes people give for joining a class.

C Houle[2] divides motivation into three broad categories. Accordingly, learners can be one of the following:

- goal-orientated

  they are learning to gain specific objectives; they have a fairly clear-cut purpose in attending a class.

- activity-orientated

  they are interested in the activity itself; they like sharing learning and being members of a group.

- learning-orientated

  they are interested in learning for its own sake; they have a fundamental desire to know and to grow through learning.

It needs to be remembered, though, that these are not finite categories but overlapping ones.

At present there is a trend towards the first of Houle's categories, with vocational courses becoming more important to people. A survey carried out by HMI[3] in 1987 of 34 institutions, which included some further education colleges, classified 30% of adult education courses as vocational. The higher figure for the vocationally orientated courses may not be entirely due to the inclusion of further education colleges in the survey, as the trend towards certificated courses is noted elsewhere. The move towards ever closer European co-operation is supporting this, and increased personal links, formed through business, family or friendship are part of the same process. The European world is getting smaller.

Most learners, then, have several reasons for wanting to learn a foreign language. In addition, these reasons will vary, at least partly, according to the nature of the institution, the courses on offer and the locality. A survey of 410 adult education students in a London college undertaken in 1990 found that 34% had joined because they had friends or relatives speaking the foreign language. While 74% enjoyed the intellectual stimulation a foreign language course offers, and 93% liked a sense of challenge, only 27% had joined primarily for holiday reasons. 50% of those questioned, on the other hand, had given work-related reasons and an astonishing 80% wanted to prepare for an examination towards the end of the course[4].

These findings, however, are in contrast to a survey undertaken throughout Lancashire in the same year, where 473 adults were asked to give their reasons for joining a foreign language course. Here 80% gave holiday reasons as the main motive, 61% wanted to keep their minds alert, 26% liked to have a pleasant evening out, 24% only were interested in qualifications, 23% had joined for work reasons and 23% had friends or relatives who spoke the same language[5].

There are a number of points to note in relation to students' reasons for joining a class, which are of importance to the tutor. The first is that the initial motivation which students have will vary, and this variation needs to be taken into account in the development of the course. Secondly, the motivation to continue learning does not come from quite the same source as the motivation to start. Persevering in learning - which is one of the characteristics of the good language learner[6] - is a combination of a great many things. One study divided motivation into two aspects: *an 'instrumental' outlook, reflecting the practical value and advantages of learning a new language, and an 'integrative' outlook, reflecting a sincere and personal interest in the people and culture*[7]. The integrative attitude is the one which appears to *sustain better the long-term motivation*[7], making the student more open, receptive and even able to retain and use the language better. Motivation is also sustained by success, which is something well within the control of the tutor in the methods and materials adopted; we all know for example how *students too readily slip into disillusionment and consequent failure because the range of demands is too great*[8].

The tutor therefore has a crucial role in sustaining motivation for the *very demanding task of second language learning*[7] and in order to achieve this will need to take heed of many social and psychological factors which affect the students in their group. Students come to classes with characteristics which may help or hinder themselves and others. *Each group has a historical background, or lack of it, which includes its behaviour*[9] and each individual arrives with *a package of experiences and values*[10], which includes expectations about the tutor, about learning, about certificates, about other students, about being clever or not and so on. What sort of attitudes and expectations do students have?

A most powerful expectation is connected with previous experience of education, a process which, for most of us, makes a deep impression at a time when we are young and relatively powerless.

**Students'
expectations
and attitudes**

The length of time spent in formal education varies considerably between people. For some it can be as long as twenty years, while for others it can be less than half that time. So while some class members will have an easy familiarity with teachers and with the jargon of education, and are familiar with or able to cope with new concepts, e.g. 'verbs, nouns, adjectives', for others this will perhaps be long forgotten or even unexplored territory, of not very great importance to them. Furthermore, the actual experience of learning will have been more successful for some than for others, who may look back on their school days without a great sense of having understood much. The important point to remember here is that, regardless of how successful people may have been in life, the 'return to school' will bring back a range of positive and negative feelings depending on the quality of their experience of school. Even successful and fulfilled students can feel uneasy when confronted with 'educated' people, or with the feeling of being back at square one. We will look at this a little more closely in unit 2 when considering drop-out, which is often the result of stress and personal or job-related problems.

Whether the student has studied a language before and what the experience was like will also play a part. Perhaps it lasted only one or two years; perhaps the student was not able to take any examination; perhaps it lasted as long as eight years and was successful and pleasurable; perhaps the language was studied but never ever spoken in class. Students may find, for example, that their experience and expectation of not saying much in class is disturbed in a communicatively orientated classroom, leaving them disconcerted by a new methodology and by demands which they perceive as considerable. For others this may pose no problem whatsoever.

Educational experience will have equipped some students, but not all, to study alone. Those who are used to formal study will have developed their own patterns of study and of recording their learning; those with shorter educational experience may find the return to learning difficult, and hence risk obtaining less from the course than their abilities would warrant.

Learners also have expectations about how a tutor will view them and behave towards them and will have feelings about what their relationship to the tutor should be. Students often refer to the tutor as 'the teacher' for example. *As soon as tutor and students encounter each other ... mutual sets of expectations about personal behaviour begin to hold sway*[11]. Groups automatically invest the tutor with authority, and each student's view of that is very personal. Depending upon their personality and experience, both in the family and at school, students will expect to be taught or to learn in certain ways. They may expect to participate and be disappointed and frustrated if no opportunity is given; they may, on the other hand, be anxious about participation and expect to be very tutor-led. Some may see the tutor as a learning resource, whom they can use, while others may see him or her as distant and rather elevated - 'may I ask a question, please?'

Tutors need to be aware that the language class does have certain characteristics which can easily increase unease. Firstly, in Keep Fit or Yoga classes the class does things simultaneously, so that no-one stands out, whereas in pottery, by contrast, the student can work alone with occasional advice. The student in the language class, however, often performs alone and in public. For adults this is a source of anxiety which we shall consider further in unit 2. Secondly, as Stern[12] points out, the learner will feel some disorientation and loss of status because he or she cannot act without help (is therefore back in the position of a child) and, we could add, will probably act imperfectly when he or she does speak.

So, there are some powerful psychological attitudes which adult students have to cope with and which they bring to learning. The tutor should be aware of this in his or her approach.

We have seen that adults bring to a class expectations which originate in their formal education or their personal lives. They also bring formed habits. Each of us, in our own way and in our own terms, develops strategies to cope with the demands and opportunities of life; when these habits are challenged or shown to be unsuccessful in some particular way we may react strongly to protect our habit, or we may open ourselves to a new strategy. Anxiety is likely. Gwynneth Griffiths, a person with long educational experience, noted her reactions to joining an adult class. *I am worried that my old ways of behaving will not be acceptable - to others or to me - and I am not sure I will be able to 'perform' in a new way*[13], she wrote in her diary.

Stern points out that *language learning often involves strong positive or negative emotions*[14]. Faced with the stress of new learning students can retreat into silence, theoretical learning, cease to pay attention, deflect attention to others or to another subject, joke, etc. It takes a skilled tutor to recognise this behaviour and assist students around such blocks to learning.

A third important element in adult education, in addition to motivation and expectations, is age. It is important in many respects - stage of life, confidence, faculties. To some extent age correlates with types of motivation. Older people will join a class less for instrumental reasons than for expressive (or integrative) ones[15]; younger people may be more likely to need a language for their job, for instance. From the tutor's point of view the issue of age may be connected more with the benefits to a group of having a good mix, but he or she will also need to understand the feelings and learning patterns of people in different age groups.

Age

There is no hard evidence that ability to learn languages is less good among adults than in children. *No age stands out as optimal or critical for all aspects of second language learning*[16]. The evidence is rather that older learners can benefit more than young children from cognitive approaches, that is, those approaches which include some explanation or study of the language itself. The issues connected with age in the language class are, however, more those of subjective feeling and of pressures on the individual. People in their middle years may have many competing claims on their time both at home and at work, and may possibly feel more threatened by failure. Older people may be more relaxed in learning, though they may have subjective feelings about, say, their memory deteriorating. While their memory may, in fact, be better than that of some younger people, their awareness of changes in themselves may affect their confidence.

The range of ability in relation to language learning in a normal class is usually more significant than the issue of age. Older people may not hear as well as others and feel a little silly as a result, as deafness is often mistaken for a lack of understanding, even in conversation in one's native language; this problem is increased in the foreign language class.

Summary

Adult students have a variety of motivations for attending a class. They come with certain abilities and intentions and will have expectations about the process, the tutor and their relationship to others. Some of these expectations will contribute to their learning, while others will hinder it. The class may be a very important part of their week, or it may be one of a number of other activities.

In his or her relationship with the class, the tutor should be aware of these varying perspectives and learn how to respond to student needs, which are discussed in unit 2.

References

1. DES, *Education and training for the 21st Century. Vol. 2. The challenge to colleges*, para. 3.6 (Cm 1536 Vol. II), HMSO (1991).

2. Houle, C, in Cross, K P, *Adults as learners*, Jossey-Bass (1986).

3. DES, *A survey of foreign language courses for adult students in 34 institutions*, a report by HMI, para. 2.3, DES (1988).

4. Arthur, L, *Study into independent language learning*, Goldsmiths' College (1990).

5. Ainslie, S, *Foreign language courses for adults - the Lancashire survey*, Hugh Baird College, Bootle (1990).

6. Stern, H H, *Fundamental concepts of language teaching*, OUP (1983).

7. Gardner, R C and W E Lambert, *Attitudes and motivation in second language learning*, Newbury House (1972), p 132.

8. Jaques, D, *Learning in groups*, Croom Helm (1984), p 44.

9. Jaques, see (8), p 21.

10. Rogers, A, *Teaching adults*, Open University (1986).

11. Jaques, see (8), p 145.

12. Stern, see (6), p 382.

13. Griffiths, G, Chapter 4: *Images of interdependence: authority and power in teaching/learning*, in Boud, D and V Griffin (eds), *Appreciating adults learning; from the learners' perspective*, Kogan Page (1988).

14. Stern, see (6), p 375.

15. Rogers, see (10).

16. Stern, see (6).

1. a. Make a list of the purposes which you believe your students have in joining a class.
    b. Check your list with them and see how accurate your assessment was.

2. a. Consider the members of your class in terms of the length of their formal education, as far as you know it.
    b. Do you believe it affects their approach to language learning?
    c. If so, how?

3. a. What is the age span of your class?
    b. Can you detect approaches to learning which you feel may be age-related?
    c. What are they?

Unit 2

Recognising the learner's needs

Duncan Sidwell

This unit discusses the varied needs which adult language learners have and how, if not met, they can become barriers to learning.

The student at the centre of the learning process

There has been a considerable shift of emphasis in recent years towards putting the learner's needs at the centre of the teaching/learning process. We have come to see teaching as a process which facilitates the learning which students wish to achieve. This has not always been the case; teaching has been identified with and, in some cases, supportive of authoritarian and hierarchical systems. We can also say that the processes by which learning is facilitated need to be informed by constant feedback between the student and the tutor, and by a mutual adaptation of behaviour based on students' needs, wants and expectations.

One way of approaching the question of student needs is to consider access to good learning and teaching as a student entitlement. This goes beyond the classroom, of course. In a pluralistic and multicultural society, where literacy, access to information and the acquisition of skills enable people to participate and contribute more fully, the entitlement to take a full part should be recognised. Equal opportunity policies and open access are a reflection of this awareness. Increasing professionalism in the adult education service brings with it a recognition of the student as a client who will have very individual needs, willing to make a personal and financial commitment in order to join a course. For many members of our society approaching an institution of learning contains no threat, of course, but for others it may well represent a big step.

Needs are not only recognised by the student. The student will be aware of some, and his or her degree of awareness will depend on personal, social and educational factors. It is the job of the tutor and others in the adult education world to spot and respond to needs and to help the student become clearer about what he or she wants. A student may want to learn a language, for example, but may not have thought out what this will involve and what aspects will be important. Other needs may be connected with the student's personality, a desire to participate, a need to be taken seriously, and so on, which he or she may not be entirely conscious of. If there is a dialogue between the tutor and student there is every likelihood that such needs can be recognised. The tutor should help the student extend his or her self-reliance and perception wherever possible.

The importance of being aware of others' needs is that unless they are recognised they can create barriers to learning of an institutional, pedagogical, social or personal nature. It may be helpful therefore to look at student needs bearing these four categories in mind. They overlap somewhat, and will be looked at here from the perspective of the potential language learner.

When a person has decided to seek a language course he or she may well approach the local college. What happens next has much to do with the professionalism of the relationship between the tutors and the head of centre. An HMI report on a number of centres drew attention to the strong connection between quality of provision and close contact between language teaching staff and the head of centre. Referring to provision and the recruitment of teachers, the report says that *in all institutions where staff with foreign language expertise were consulted at least three-quarters of the work was judged satisfactory or better, and in several the proportion of good or satisfactory work was much higher*[1]. This contrasted with those institutions where contact was lacking. This sort of professional dialogue within centres affects what happens from initial contact to the outcome in the classroom.

Needs which may be catered for at the level of the institution

The written information provided can be supplemented by personal contact at enrolment time, when questions relating to the course and other questions can be raised. Just how enrolment is organised varies from institution to institution. Not all tutors will have the chance to meet their new students before the beginning of a course. Some adult education centres have special enrolment days, others have open days or open sessions in addition to a telephone advice service. Others have introduced a more formal initial language assessment test or a student profiling system where, for example, previous achievements and learning experiences may be taken into account. Each institute will have its own procedures of which the new tutor ought to be aware.

Before enrolment, however, potential students need information. They are entitled to a specification which includes details of the purpose, level and content of the courses. In order to provide this, the centre and the tutors together need to have worked out their aims and objectives, something which HMI[2] have noted as being generally lacking and in need of attention. Students may also require some guidance as to which course or level is appropriate for them and here it is helpful to devise (or use existing) descriptions of levels. A number of organisations have developed their own system of levels. The Council of Europe has published Threshold Levels in a number of languages, and an intermediary objective below that level is called *Waystage*. The Royal Society of Arts, the Institute of Linguists and the newer National Council for Vocational Qualifications publish target levels of attainment. These are all useful for reference purposes in helping to design course specifications. The HMI report referred to above underlines the inadequacy of many arrangements for matching students to courses: it is scarcely satisfactory that *in many institutions students more or less decide for themselves which levels they are at* without guidance, or that *in eight of the major institutions inspected the stated aims of the courses were too brief to be helpful*[3]. It is of course possible to offer good written descriptions and to investigate ways of assisting students to make the best choice.

Since the principal aim of students is to be able to speak the target language[4], the course description should be framed in terms of competencies; it should give an idea of what students may expect to be able **to do** at the end of a course. There are implications in this for the method of teaching and for the materials used, because if these do not bring the students to perform communicatively, the course specification will be misleading. For this reason some indication should be given about methodology, including what will not be done or expected. As we have seen, educational methods change and students need to know in what way.

Assessing language learning needs

Whichever system for enrolling new students into new courses may be used, students and tutors alike face the difficulty of knowing what kind of class may be the right one. At times practical reasons force decisions, such as 'Beginners Arabic' takes place only on a Tuesday night. Other determinants are more complex. Foreign language classes may be graded into 'Beginners', 'Intermediate' or 'Advanced' - though often what is meant by these categories is less than clear.

In many instances adults will have learnt some of the language somewhere else, be it at school, in adult education classes, on their own through self-study or simply because they have spent some time in the country of the language concerned. No doubt most will have forgotten a lot and many would like to start from scratch, even if they are not absolute beginners.

Their linguistic needs may be just as varied. Some may need mainly speaking and listening skills, others may have to learn to read or write for particular purposes. Others may need informal language mainly for social interaction rather than the more formal language required for work purposes. Alternatively, they may be more interested in cultural aspects of language learning rather than the strictly functional ones. Furthermore, many adults have parents whose first language is not English. They may have learnt colloquial language informally in the home environment and would like to concentrate on accuracy and written skills in the classroom context.

When advising learners to choose the right class, previous language learning experiences and communication skills in the target language will have to be taken into account. The latter may range from the ability to utter a few survival statements to being able to maintain a simple conversation, to convey messages in the past and/or future tense, and the use of social and strategic skills such as asking for repetition to clarify messages.

The person advising the learner to choose the right class, however, will not only look at the language level competencies but also, as mentioned before, consider other factors such as convenience, accessibility, financial commitment, amount of time available to study, the amount of time of study support needed, and the matching of the teaching and learning styles of the individuals concerned. After all, all learning involves the whole being, not only our intellectual functions but also our senses and physical well-being.

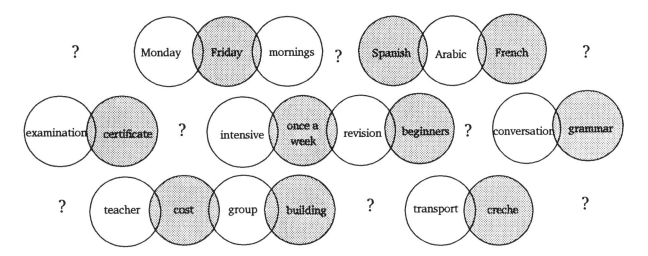

The previous section touched on some of these needs - the need to co-operate and the need to succeed being two of them. Just as you need to feel physically comfortable in a classroom, so you need to feel psychologically comfortable. Maslow[5] relates this to the absence of fear; and this is not too strong a word to use in relation to the emotion many people feel when having to speak in a language class. Feeling good is a major learning need. It has even been suggested that *the affective (i.e. emotional) component contributes at least as much as and often more to language learning than the cognitive skills*[6].

Drop-out from language classes is slightly higher than that from the generality of courses[7] and may occur for many reasons. Outside pressures on students undoubtedly play a part - moving house, work, family commitments, etc - and there are also other reasons to do with organisation, methodology, group composition etc. In the 42 cases of drop-out which were followed up in detail in one survey[8], various reasons for leaving the class were given, but many ex-students went on to confess in conversation that actually they had feelings of inadequacy in the classroom which they could not handle. People who are successful and confident in their daily lives can find the stress of not being sure of themselves too much. *When you are like me - I am 52 - and you are well on in your job, you don't like making mistakes in front of people. I only missed one lesson in fact - I felt very nervous about going back. I was a bit too embarrassed to start talking, which is what I really wanted.* (Respondents in conversation with writer)[9]. Of course, people leave all types of classes for many reasons, but indications are that the drop-out rate from language classes is higher than from others, and anxiety may well be a reason.

Anxiety may also be socially based and prove a barrier. Participants in adult education - and particularly in language classes - tend to come from higher socio-economic groups. This can be experienced as a barrier. *The others were more professional people - I didn't have the courage to go again*[10]. No doubt no-one intended this, but had the tutor spotted this student's feelings, she might not have left the class.

Needs which relate to social and psychological factors

**The teaching/
learning
process**

In answering students' needs in relation to the process of learning and teaching, a methodology should aim to achieve the following.

- The methods used should promote the aims of the course. Students who enrol with the aim of learning to speak the target language become frustrated if they do not spend a considerable time listening and speaking communicatively. Reading a text and answering questions on it or talking in their native language is not what they come for.
  What is heard, spoken and read should correspond to the elements of the syllabus.

- Students should find the methods used enjoyable; they should derive pleasure from doing the learning tasks.

- The method should provide feedback on progress. There should be an 'I can do...' reminder every now and then, which can take the form of a task to be completed. Such tasks can be as simple as asking the way, or more complex interactions involving negotiation or explanation. Such benchmarks of success and competence are major motivators. Too often tutors move on to other content areas without ensuring that the students **themselves** are satisfied that they can perform the necessary language, rather than just knowing it.
  Many students actually like such informal assessments. There is evidence that they provide motivation and a reason for learning for many of them. As the quality of formal assessments continues to improve we may expect interest in them to increase also.

- Tasks should be within the competence of the learners and lead them to a feeling of mastery and success.

- Materials should be varied. Students learn through different senses. Some are more visually orientated than others; some have good auditory perception and retention; some retain the written word particularly well.

- The method should promote student needs for autonomy in learning. It should seek to provide them with techniques and confidence to pursue their studies by self-access. This may be as simple as suggesting homework, or may involve a discussion with a group of students about how people can help themselves.

- The method should respond to students' need to contribute. Students often have excellent ideas about how to extend or adapt materials, for example, and this participation also promotes their own thinking about the process of learning.

Students' awareness of their needs in relation to methods of teaching and learning will vary considerably, depending on how much experience they have in education and how much experience they have of communicative language teaching. Students may well have negative preferences because of bad experiences or learning difficulties in the past. One of the tutor's functions is to balance what he or she chooses as an activity necessary to achieve a particular aim, with feedback from students about how far it helps them.

We have discussed motivation in unit 1 and have mentioned the unconscious needs of students which play a part in their behaviour. These unconscious motivations may be quite powerful and can even destabilise a group. They can be very varied. They may include a drive to succeed and reveal elements of competitiveness. They may be social and involve seeking friends. They may include a desire to please. While it is not the tutor's responsibility to respond to all needs of this sort, they do have to be recognised as part of the dynamic of the group. They can, of course, be turned to good use. Co-operative activities give space for friendly emotions to be expressed and opportunity to get to know each other. Using the unconscious motivations of a group in building on the combined resources tends to increase satisfaction.

Perhaps the whole question of needs can be brought together under the general heading of personal satisfaction. In one survey one third of potential adult learners gave personal satisfaction as the main reason for learning[11]. Unless learners do feel generally satisfied in their learning, what has been achieved?

The next section will examine some ways in which learner satisfaction with the process of learning can be enhanced.

References

1. DES, *A survey of foreign language courses for adult students in 34 institutions*, a report by HMI, para. 3.9, DES (1988).

2. DES, *Education for adults*, a review by HMI, paras. 59, 60, HMSO (1991).

3. DES (1988), see (2), paras. 3.6, 3.7.

4. Sidwell, D, 'A survey of modern language classes in adult education', in *Adult Education*, Vol. 52, No. 5 (January 1980).

5. Maslow, A H, 'Defence and Growth' in Silberman, M L (ed), *The psychology of open teaching and learning*, Little Barn (1972).

6. Stern, H H, *Fundamental concepts of language teaching*, OUP (1983).

7. Sidwell, see (4).

8. Sidwell, see (4).

9. Sidwell, see (4).

10. Sidwell, see (4).

11. Cross, K P, *Adults as learners*, Jossey-Bass (1986).

1.   a. Discuss with students their views on:

- the conditions required for language learning;
- the conditions which most promote their learning;
- the use of the tape recorder and the OHP;
- the tutor behaviour they find most helpful;
- what makes them anxious in class.

This activity may also be carried out by asking students to get into groups of two or three and then discuss the questions. If they are anxious about speaking in public, they are not likely to say this in a large group.

2.   a. Consider the students in your class.
     b. What do you believe to be some of the unconscious motivations?

Unit 3

Facilitating the learning

Duncan Sidwell

This unit considers ways in which tutors can enhance the learning by a student-centred attitude, by using appropriate teaching techniques and classroom management.

The learning climate

We have seen in the first two units how adults come to classes with considerable life experience to contribute, with intentions and expectations and with conscious and unconscious motivations. Any of these may help or hinder them in their learning. While adult students vary considerably in these things, they also have in common a desire to learn, and one function of the tutor is to assist them, while taking into account the individual variations in attitude and need. The tutor carries a major responsibility to create a helpful learning climate and we can consider how this can be achieved under four headings:

★ A learner-centred approach
★ Teaching techniques
★ Group psychology
★ The reflective and self-developing tutor

Learner-centred approach

The psychologist Carl Rogers has pointed out that we cannot teach a person anything directly; we can only facilitate his or her learning.

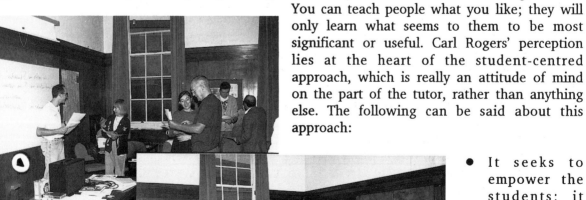

You can teach people what you like; they will only learn what seems to them to be most significant or useful. Carl Rogers' perception lies at the heart of the student-centred approach, which is really an attitude of mind on the part of the tutor, rather than anything else. The following can be said about this approach:

● It seeks to empower the students; it increases their capacity, feelings of strength and self-respect.

- It recognises that students will learn in different ways and it encourages them to follow their own best strategy.

- The input fits the students' needs, wishes and capabilities.

- Learning takes students into partnership.

- The role of the tutor is to recognise growth points and to facilitate their development.

A learner-centred approach may be something which students themselves are not used to, and it is possible that they will feel uncomfortable with it at times. Experienced tutors will know that some students like the tutor to tell them what's what, and that they may feel uneasy with a method which requires them to do some exploring for themselves. One of the tutor's functions is to take the student a little further.

In language teaching there are two very clear aspects for the student-centred focus: the syllabus and the methodology. In each case the learning will be facilitated if the tutor adopts an approach which is flexible in its response to student preferences.

Learner-centred language teaching

We have enough knowledge of student needs in general to construct practically orientated communicative language syllabuses. There has to be room for local variation, and it is important that the syllabuses developed by tutors take account of student wishes where appropriate. It is not possible or desirable to discuss the whole of a syllabus with a class, but amendments can be made. For example, students may say they want to be able to talk more about what they have been doing and for this they will need particular structures, or they may feel the need to use question forms more, and so on. They may also welcome a session devoted to some aspect of the country whose language they are learning, or have the opportunity to meet a group of native speakers.

It is, however, in the methodology that particular flexibility is needed. An underlying objective should be to enable students to be active in their study and to learn to seek out ways of improving their command of the language. They will almost certainly need encouragement to be adventurous, to try to communicate with inadequate language and not to be discouraged, to use reference material and to find ways of practising between sessions which suit them. In order to feel empowered to do so they should enjoy a methodology which concentrates on getting them to perform, enabling them to do something which they perceive as useful. This can be a most difficult thing for a tutor to achieve, because adults will at times take refuge in seeking to talk about language rather than actually performing it. Language learning is actually a **performance subject** much like dance, and the tutor's role is to give opportunities to perform creatively. Knowing about dance does not enable you to dance.

Because language learning raises quite strong feelings, as we have seen, it is advisable to approach discussion about methodology with caution. Learners may be experiencing some techniques for the first time, and they may be unsure about them as well as unsure in themselves. Discussion may lead to strongly held positions which are unhelpful for progression in the long run. It is best, therefore, to obtain feedback gradually, particularly once people have got to know each other and after activities they have enjoyed. It is also good to involve them in the development of materials, as this increases their sense of participation, usually produces good ideas and develops their own autonomy and consciousness of language learning processes.

Developing teaching strategies

Language learning in the classroom necessarily depends quite heavily on the tutor. While the syllabus or course content should be adjusted to the needs of adult learners, and teaching methods employed should be geared to adults, that is learner-centred, the teacher nevertheless provides the input and takes the lead in the structuring of the learning process as part of his/her professional responsibilities towards the learner. A considerable amount of work has been done to define tutor-led strategies such as those below which enhance this particular process and make the learning more effective[1].

- Structure the learning. This does not mean following a grammatical syllabus! What it means is that the material which learners encounter should be coherent and meaningful, with supporting interconnections made clear. It also implies careful attention to gradation of difficulty.

- Take small steps and allow for brisk pace. In language learning it is easy to be overwhelmed and the various skills are best acquired by breaking down the larger task into meaningful smaller activities. By taking small and achievable steps at a reasonable pace students will become conscious of their own abilities.

- Provide redundant information and many examples. Language learners need to experience a great deal of the target language - much more than they will actually use. In part this is to acquaint them with the sounds. It is also to enable them to distinguish particular new language items among others. Reading is very helpful. It is therefore a good idea to include the particular point being studied with other material, increasing the complexity of the examples as appropriate. It is rather like making a cake: you gradually stir in the various ingredients; putting them all in at the same time does not make for a good cake and you risk indigestion. The use of the foreign language in the class-room by the tutor is also very relevant here. Tutors need not worry if some of what they say in class is not understood by students - provided the main message is understood and students do not feel too left out. The practice of using a great deal of the foreign language in the classroom is much to be recommended. It gives many other learning possibilities for different students as they pick up words and expressions.

- Give feedback and corrections, particularly at first. In language learning too much 'correction' can be avoided by good initial listening and practice and by ensuring that students have 'got it'. Tutors should beware of the danger of allowing students to form bad habits, which are difficult to change later.

- Get 80% accuracy early. This is bound up with the above points. It is important for a feeling of success that small amounts of input should be quickly mastered. Only in this way can learners cope with the next task.

- Promote continuous student practice. You do not acquire skills by being **told** how to do something. You have to do it and do it frequently. All lessons need therefore to have a rhythm of presentation, practice and use, with this rhythm occurring several times during the session. Student practice is the principal component in creating success.

There are other aspects of teaching which can be added to this list.

- If something is not working, drop it. There may be many reasons why an activity fails. Difficulty, level, tiredness, etc can all play their part. Once you have recognised this, to continue is only reinforcing failure.

- Re-use previously learned material constantly. This not only provides practice but also gives students an experience of success. It is a useful energiser (for weary workers) and most helpful in learning if the first few minutes of a lesson are used to revise recently acquired language.

- Create a foreign language atmosphere, partly by using the language extensively yourself and also by decorating the room appropriately, inviting native speakers to the class where possible, etc. (See unit 7 for further teaching strategies.)

The group itself

No two groups are the same and the way in which a tutor manages interaction will depend on the natures of the participants. However, although made up of different individuals, groups do have certain definable characteristics and behaviours[2]. The principal feature of any group is that it will work on at least two levels. It will have a task to perform (e.g. learn the language), which is its purpose, and at the same time there will be feelings about the task, about the tutor and about the other members of the group which will influence how that task is performed. These feelings may well be as important, or even more important to the members than the task itself, and if emotional satisfaction is not obtained, the task may not be well performed and a good feeling will not be experienced about the task itself. Negative feelings about learning tasks inhibit the learning and the retention of language. What are some of these non-task factors?

Individuals will view the tutor differently, but the group as a whole will look to him or her for a lead. The way this is handled is critical for the health of the group and a sharing of authority by the leader - through the distribution of tasks, the acknowledgement of expertise and ensuring wide participation - will contribute to ease of feeling. Individual views of how a tutor should behave will be projected onto the tutor, and this will be particularly strong at the beginning, before people have had time to get to know each other.

The group is likely to move through phases as individuals move out from themselves towards others, encounter them and feel the resulting tension, and finally seek to resolve those tensions amicably as they come to appreciate each other and develop what is known as a 'we feeling'. The tutor again has a role in managing this, by being appreciative and allowing the sub-groups, which will possibly form, space to perform tasks without excluding others. The group will not remain static in its internal relationships, nor in its learning processes. These should develop along with other aspects of group life.

Groups will look to the tutor to set some forms of standards or patterns. This has a number of functions: it gives people a sense of security, it vests the power of 'holding the ring' in the hands of the institutional leader, and it allows people to relax. Standards may include many unsaid things, such as not interrupting, waiting while people have a go at saying something, not laughing unkindly at mistakes, keeping on task, etc. Patterns are important, such as regularity of time keeping and regular spots during which the students can talk to the tutor about any aspect of their own study. Learning itself may be taken to be a co-operative activity. Working partners may be varied, and so on. Clearly the general manner of the tutor will heavily influence these aspects of group behaviour.

Patterns of communication will develop. Eye contact in groups is rarely if ever random, and can be used as much to exclude as to include members. The same applies to language use and to whom it is directed. It is quite normal for some people not to be spoken to and not to have much chance to talk. Co-operative attitudes fostered by the tutor and deliberate attention to certain members can serve as a reminder to everyone that the whole class is involved.

It is important that the tutor should not merely be aware of these dynamics but should foster the healthy aspects of group life. He or she should also develop a repertoire of approaches so as to encourage different learning styles, give varied stimuli, teach learners the value of flexible learning and keep everyone alert. Some general suggestions are given here about atmosphere creation.

- Initial contact sets the tone for the course and should be warm, friendly and businesslike. The first few sessions are critical in establishing confidence and building a learning community. It helps to get to know students, following their progress and helping them catch up when necessary.

- Be businesslike. Students have paid for a course and do not like to have time wasted. Engage students rapidly in interactive activities, as this will not only establish contact but also establish expectations. Even in the first session of a language they can practise greetings, ask each other's names and find out where others live.

- Reduce competition by selecting activities which require co-operation. Pair and group work helps to reduce public stress and enhance fellow feeling. React with pleasure to success, be relaxed about inaccuracies and help the shy to come forward.

Fundamental to the good learning atmosphere is the need to promote the development of trust, respect and caring among group members[3]. The types of activity you choose and your manner will tend either to bring this about or to diminish its likelihood. Your language will affect this too, of course. Language can have the effect of holding people away as much as reassuring them, and straightforward language which avoids jargon makes listeners feel more comfortable.

The reflective and self-developing tutor

In some adult education centres it is possible for tutors to get together and exchange ideas. These meetings provide an opportunity to develop teaching methodology and to bring tutors into contact with new perceptions and techniques. It is of great value for tutors to see each other teach and to reflect on their own practice. All tutors can become better at what they do and see ever more possibilities. In part this must come from discussion with students about the techniques, conditions and tutor behaviour which are most helpful, but in part it can come from the tutor alone or, preferably, a tutor working with a colleague and looking at the student's learning. A group of Open University tutors has developed a sequence of questions to enable tutors to reflect on their own teaching[4]. These are as follows, and all involve watching students at work.

★ What did they do?
  Here you simply gather information on what went on for a period of time. The focus can be on one or more students.

★ What did they learn?
  Here there is some guess work! Do the students reveal any new behaviours? Do they appear to have a capability or awareness which is new to them? Did they learn things which were not intended?

★ How worthwhile was it?
  Here you judge the value of what you see, or what you have given them to do. Does it bring them nearer their goal? Could it have been more relevant to the syllabus and to student expectations?

★ What did I do?
  What effect did you (or a tutor you observed) have on the learning?

★ What did I learn?
  This draws together the answers to the other questions and helps formulate the answer to question 6.

★ What do I intend to do now? How will I plan the future in the light of the perceptions I have had?

Even if it is not possible to work with a colleague for a short while on these questions, it is possible for us to stand back from our activity periodically and put such questions to ourselves. Just as learning for students needs to be centred on their needs and perceptions, so it does for the tutor, and if in-service education is not available as readily as one would wish, it is all the more important for tutors to become reflective.

References

1. Rosenshine, B, 'Teaching functions in instructional programmes', in *Elementary School Journal* Vol. 83 No. 4 (1983).

2. Jaques, D, *Learning in groups*, Croom Helm (1984).

3. Maclean, H, Chapter 10: 'Linking person centred teaching to qualitative research training' in Boud, D and V Griffin (eds), *Appreciating adults learning; from the learners' perspective*, Kogan Page (1988).

4. Ashton, P, Hunt, P, Jones, S and G Watson, *Curriculum in action: practical classroom evaluation*, pack P533, Open University (1981).

Over to you

1. Take the six questions from p 25 and go through them in relation to your own work. If possible work on them with a colleague.

2. Discuss activities which can be used early in a language course to promote co-operation between students.

3. CILT can advise about how to obtain videos of language teaching. Watch a short clip of such a video with some colleagues and discuss the student and teacher behaviour.

4. Reflect on your own experience as a young person or as an adult. What were your feelings about the learning environment and your expectations of the teacher or tutor?

Looking at language   2

Understanding learning

Lore Arthur

This unit looks at the concept of language and languages, examines how we learn our own mother tongue, considers issues in connection with first and second language learning and aims to promote a general understanding of what is meant by language awareness.

Imagine conducting a street interview and asking the question: 'What does the word language mean?'. The answers - assuming there were any - would be both predictable and confusing. They would be diverse, complex, imprecise, bewildering or simplistic, even crude. They would, of course, depend on the individual's point of view, experience and understanding of language. Some might describe language as a tool, a means of human communication, a way of expressing our thoughts, dreams, needs and desires; an essential survival kit in an increasingly complex world. Others may speak of language in the context of art or music, refer to body language, or non-verbal communication. Ideas such as 'good' or 'bad'

What do we mean by 'language'?

language may emerge full of moral overtones and hidden class-conscious agendas. Others might see language as a coded form of utterances involving sounds, using the larynx, vocal cords and mouth; or they may refer to concepts such as grammar, structures, idioms, even semantics or lexis. In other words, clear definitions are impossible to obtain. The concept of language is too complex for any one person to grasp. There are no boundaries, no limitations, nor is there a finite entity. Language, then, is tangible and intangible at the same time. It is essentially a human form of communication because language in the form of speech is, in essence, a set of meanings, a device for expressing human thoughts based on human experiences.

> *Language is by its nature beyond the total grasp of any one human and groups of humans. It extends from the past through to the present into the future, and it extends across millions of users who will never communicate directly with each other, even if they share what is regarded as the same language.*[1]

Not all thought processes require language. After all, it is possible to use imagination or feel emotions without the use of language. We may use our whole body, that is our hands, feet, posture, facial expressions, either consciously or subconsciously to replace, add to or subtract from what we may wish to communicate through language. The articulation of language in the form of speech acts, however, requires both its production and its comprehension through sounds in spoken form or though symbols in writing. In addition, the emission of language or speech requires a sender and a receiver, even if the receiver is in some cases the self. Communication between two or more people requires an intention, a message and a means. The word 'message' refers to the content of what we wish to say and the word 'means' to the tool used for its transmission, that is the language itself. We also need a device for transmitting language. This may be either the voice in a face-to-face interaction or another text source such as reading and listening material.

The use of language, then, implies a process of transmitting and receiving information or knowledge. Knowledge, it may be argued, offers access to power and control. Our whole cultural and political systems are based on language, language used for specific purposes, language or forms of language understood by most but not necessarily by all. Language used at will and in restricted form, can both include and exclude. It can prevent us from joining social groupings, alternatively it can give us a sense of belonging.

Languages are, therefore, above all social constructs. They have evolved separately over thousands of years within natural physical boundaries or those devised by groups of communities or peoples. They have been, and continue to be, a contributory factor if not the cause, as well as solution, of conflict and strife as an expression of needs, beliefs, ideals and power.

Language as a field of study

Yet since the beginning of human existence hundreds even thousands of languages or speech communities have come and gone. We can deduce this from the fact that 2,769 languages are spoken around the world today - depending on what you count as a language[2]. The origins of our own linguistic civilisation can be traced back to the Classical Sanskrit of India and the group of Indo-European languages with common ancestral language families such as Latin, Greek, Celtic, Germanic and Slavonic and their related cousins whose descendants comprise the major languages of the northern part of the Indian subcontinent including Panjabi, Gujerati, Bengali, Urdu and Hindi. The kinship of languages has occupied scholars, notably the Brothers Grimm, for centuries.

The study of language itself, that is linguistics, is relatively new. It does not comprise one agreed view but rather a variety of competing views, or distinct schools and movements. These seek to examine either components of language, such as language pattern in spoken and written language, the sounds of language, varieties of language - that is social, regional dialects and accents, or, alternatively, its social role and functions, discourse and register, and the world of meanings or semantics. Language then can be grouped into:

★ sound systems (intonation, stress, rhythm, pause, elision, vowels, consonants)

★ grammar systems (inflection for plurality, tense, possession, word order etc)

★ lexical systems (expressions, words such as nouns, verbs, adjectives, pronouns, etc)

★ culture systems (language in social context, gestures, social habits and values)

These groupings raise questions about how language works, what it consists of, what it means and how it is used, for which purpose, in which context and situation, and, above all, how language is learnt, both our mother tongue and a second/foreign language.

How do we learn languages?

To begin with, there is nothing difficult or obscure about speaking and understanding language - that is, at least our own mother tongue. Given normal circumstances we all have the innate ability to learn at least one language, that is the language of our social, cultural environment - our mother tongue. We simply need to make use of our brain. The brain, however, is somewhat exceptional and unique. It is able to store an unlimited amount of information for years, even for decades. It can adjust this information, conceptualise it, connect new learning with past events, draw conclusions and constantly add to our existing knowledge.

In addition, the production and reception of language involves other parts of the human body. With speech, for example, air is pushed through the lungs, the windpipe, the larynx, the glottis (the space between the vocal cords) as well as the oral tract, which is the air passage offered by the mouth, and the nasal tract, which is the air passage offered by the nose. Each speech community will use these available tools to produce either voiceless or voiced sounds controlled by the brain. The auditory or visual perception of language, too, depends on the functioning of our ears or vision. The meaning we put to these symbols, however, involves the brain and some of our muscles[3].

We may understand, at least to some degree, the physical functioning of language. Yet how precisely we manage to **learn** a language is less clear. There are those who maintain that human beings are born with an innate ability to grasp regularities in language forms, that is grammar, common to all languages. Theorists such as Chomsky refer to the Language Acquisition Device (LAD). Accordingly, all children, except those with physical or mental disabilities, can learn language with equal success. Educators will argue that more than innate ability is required to master language - a process which, after all, takes several years. The environment, social conditioning, nurture rather than nature aspects are of greater significance and conducive to learning. Hawkins[4], for example, stresses the importance of 'adult time' in the development of language. This is the amount of time children have as individuals in dialogue with adults which will enable them to develop language and above all thought processes. How we learn language, then, is likely to be a combination of our innate abilities, of which little is known, and our social environment, the attention and care we give to its development.

Language learning as a lifelong process

We may not yet fully understand what enables human beings to learn a language. Yet only exceptional circumstances will prevent children learning to speak remarkably quickly. Over two hundred years of research have shown that there are certain age-related stages within normal language development; for example, 'cooing' and 'babbling' to the one word and two word stages among babies and young infants. At the age of four they will be able to form plurals and past tenses. Such progress continues so that by the time they are four or five most children in all cultures studied to date can use complex co-ordinated sentences. In addition, children learn to interpret, conceptualise, connect, discard and refer to past and future events and generally develop their mental abilities in an age-related sequence, according to Piaget.

The overwhelming weight of evidence shows that the learning of our mother tongue continues, at least in some aspects, until middle and old age in a natural, almost unnoticed fashion as long as one is interested in new things. For older second language learners the picture changes slightly. While pronunciation skills as well as the ability to distinguish rapidly-spoken new sounds may decline, other skills such as reading and writing as well as a desire for grammatical accuracy may increase. In general, however, there is little empirical evidence to suggest that with increasing age language learners are disadvantaged, though their learning styles may differ[5].

Language acquisition/ second language learning

Language learning, then, is a natural part of our human existence. We may grow up being monolingual, bilingual or, indeed, multilingual depending on our cultural environment. Many British citizens of ethnic minority origin speak more than one language. The ILEA languages survey of 1987 traces 172 languages spoken by its school children at home[6]. A Sylheti speaker, for example, is likely to speak Bengali and perhaps Urdu, quite apart from English. Indeed, half the world's population is bilingual. Pluralingualism, too, is not uncommon in many Asian and African countries and some European ones.

In all societies one or more languages are learnt from early childhood in a naturalistic manner, without conscious effort as part of formal language instruction. Similarly, a newcomer to a country may, over a period of time, learn subconsciously the language of the host country, acquire new words and structures as well as an understanding of grammatical correctness and its idiomatic use. This happens regardless of whether or not the newcomer has previously acquired the language in a formal setting.

A distinction has to be made at this point between the learning of our mother tongue or first language (L1), and that of the other, the second, foreign or target language (L2). In addition, we need to differentiate between learning a language more or less subconsciously as part of our home environment (first language acquisition) and the conscious, often formal process, either within an educational institution or by self-study (second language acquisition or learning).

For the adult foreign language learner within an adult education environment, this subconscious process is seemingly much harder to achieve. He/she will learn the target language largely consciously: effort is involved in remembering words, structures, in applying forms and rules, in correcting errors both in spoken and written form. However, matters are by no means straightforward. Learning progress also occurs as a result of spontaneous, subconscious mechanisms which are activated when the learners are involved in communication in the second language[7]. Both the conscious and subconscious processes affect learners and teaching methodologies alike. Much depends on length of time and the exposure to the target language involved. Learners who learn for several hours every day over a prolonged period acquire a considerable amount of additional language without being aware of it, unlike those who hear and speak the new language for perhaps only a very limited time once a week, or even less often.

However, other factors have to be considered. These relate to the psychology of language learning, that is verbal ability, aptitude, empathy, motivation, personality, memory, learning styles, learning experiences, and the learning environment, that is where and how the learning takes place. As learners and teachers we may be interested primarily in the learning of the foreign, or second language. The relationship between our mother tongue and the new language is the one which will interest us the most. By trying to understand how our own language functions, how we communicate with each other, by learning about other languages in addition to learning to speak other languages we develop what may be referred to as 'language awareness'.

Language awareness is a person's sensitivity to and conscious awareness of the nature of language and its role in human life.[8]

References

1. McArthur, T, *A foundation course for language teachers*, CUP (1983).

2. Stevenson, V (ed), *Words: an illustrated history of western languages*, MacDonald (1983).

3. Katamba, F, *An introduction to phonology*, Longman (1989).

4. Hawkins, E, *Awareness of language*, CUP (1984).

5. Singleton, D M, *Language acquisition: the age factor*, Multilingual Matters (1989).

6. ILEA, *Languages census research and statistics*, ILEA (1987).

7. Littlewood, W, *Foreign and second language learning*, CUP (1984).

8. Donmall, B G (ed), *Language awareness*, NCLE Report No. 6. CILT (1985).

Over to you

Resources required	white box cards
Objective	to create language awareness
Activity	<ul><li>distribute cards amongst yourselves - one per person</li><li>write down how many languages you speak, even if only a little</li><li>collect cards and redistribute</li><li>write down how much you know **about** the language(s), if anything at all (country/countries where language is spoken, history, origin, anything you find worth noting)</li><li>discuss in plenum: ★ what you know and don't know ★ how languages differ ★ what languages have in common</li></ul>
Time allocated	30 minutes

Resources	pieces of blank paper, pens
Objective	to create language awareness
Activity	copy these scripts as carefully as you can then discuss your learning experience **ЧЕМПИОНАТ ЕВРОПЫ ПО ДЗЮДО** わが社のイギリス人 میرا نام عبد اللہ ہے

Group discussion	Language acquisition/Second language learning reflect/discuss: ★ how did you learn English (or another language)? - reflect on the various stages carefully ★ what was language acquisition? ★ what was second language learning? ★ can you distinguish between them? Check on your understanding of the differences and how they affect foreign language learning in the classroom.

Unit 5

Theories in language teaching

Lore Arthur

This unit looks at learning theories and language teaching methods as they relate to the adult learning situation in general and more specifically to foreign/second language teaching. Above all, the unit will consider their relevance to language teaching practices.

Why we need theories

Most good language teachers aim to:

        achieve effective communication;
        promote lively classroom interaction;
        practise one step at a time;
      arrange, if possible, furniture to create a good learning environment;
    use newspapers and other authentic materials;
   organise group and pair work;
use information gap exercises which allow the learner to think;
  create cultural awareness;
    use games, role-plays, language pattern drills or choral work to promote confidence in speaking;
      use learners' experiences and the knowledge they bring into the classroom situation;
        praise and encourage to give a sense of achievement;
        work hard to maintain the learners' motivation.

Yet all these activities, eclectic though they may seem, are embedded in one or more theoretical perspectives of which the teacher may or may not be aware. Experienced language teachers will have developed their own understanding about what they are doing within the context of the classroom. Much depends on the circumstances and people involved. Some activities may simply work better than others. Some work well with one set of learners but not with another. The reasons may not always be fully understood. Indeed, they may be too complex for any simple explanation. All language tutors, however, should have a vital concern with theory if their teaching is to avoid being aimless and purposeless[1]. In addition, understanding broad theoretical frameworks and perspectives and having an awareness of current thinking and development will give language teachers professional competence, self-assurance and equality, particularly in their relationships with other colleagues and the teaching profession in general.

There is, however, rarely just one theory; there are numerous theories and approaches. These may conflict and cause confusion. They may evolve and soon be superseded by others. Yet all theories should serve as a tool for understanding and explanation, for prediction and control of what may happen and why certain matters did or did not take place. Theories as well as methods, therefore, have a practical purpose. They centre around the **how** of teaching once the **what** and **why** have been established.

A method can be defined as a co-ordinated body of techniques and teaching procedures, related to a standard body of assumptions about the nature of language teaching.[2]

Language teaching theories and methods are, of course, not new. During the nineteenth century and well into the early part of the twentieth, foreign languages were studied largely as an intellectual discipline by analysis of their grammar and by translation. Latin was still widely used as a language of scholarship. By contrast the 'direct method' developed in the 1920s and the subsequent 'oral' and 'reading' methods tried to break new ground. These methods were not based on major linguistic theoretical perspectives; instead, they concentrated on classroom teaching practices where the emphasis was either on speaking and exclusive use of the target language or, alternatively, on reading and writing, often at the expense of the other language skills. There can still be a seductive ring to such concepts. Predictably, however, there were and are difficulties with any too dogmatically imposed and too restrictive a method which ignores the learners' needs, their cognitive abilities and individuality.

Historical perspectives

It was not until the early years of World War II that the academic study of linguistics was recognised as an important, perhaps even the most important component of language teaching[3]. Subsequent language teaching methods involved analysis of grammar and vocabulary followed by intensive oral drilling and the formation of habitual responses when speaking. Learning by habit has its roots in behaviourist psychology which in turn stems largely from experiments with animals during the latter half of the last century. The theory of classical conditioning by Pavlov (1927), for example, was based on experiments with dogs which salivated at the sound of a bell in anticipation of food. These experiments proved that animals and by implication human beings, too, can be trained by reward and punishment to respond to stimuli in a predictable way.

B F Skinner[4] transferred many of these principles to theories of language learning. His provocative book, *Verbal behaviour*, published in 1957, argued that learners, exposed to given stimuli, would learn to respond in a predictable manner. This would, eventually, lead to the formation of habits. The audio-lingual and audio-visual methods of the 1960s and early 1970s, using tapes and filmstrips respectively, relied heavily on habit formation. By repetitive drilling of non-communicative structures for the sake of grammatical accuracy, errors were eliminated, at least temporarily, and a point of saturation was reached. These methods followed fairly predictable routines which were, at times, comfortable and easy to follow. Yet they also led to paraphrasing and perhaps boredom since the learner was not an active participant in the learning process. He/she was not encouraged to use language creatively according to needs, personality and intellect.

The formation of habits

A: The beach is getting crowded now.
B: Yes, it will be more crowded tomorrow.
A: The ice-cream is very nice.
B: Yes, it will be nicer tomorrow.

1. The children are very cheerful.
2. A nice day today, isn't it?
3. The traffic is bad.
4. There are few deckchairs on the beach.
5. Isn't the water warm?

Audio-lingual method   Audio-visual method
(Una McNab, *Ealing course in German*, Longman (1969))

The situational method of about the same time, though aiming to be more realistic and student-centred, also had its limitations. By concentrating on situations, such as 'in the restaurant', language was rarely transferred in a more meaningful way outside that particular situation and rarely adapted to genuine interaction and dialogue. Emphasis was still on linguistic accuracy practised in set phrases and grammar graded in traditional sequential steps. Moreover, as Brumfit points out, situations cannot be graded. The sequencing of situations was generally random, making it *well-nigh impossible to grade structures without falsifying the situation*[5]. However, learning around situations continues to have validity in all language learning settings. Most language learners, after all, will want to use language in a variety of everyday situations such as shopping or 'ordering food in a restaurant', irrespective of current trends in teaching theory or methodology, and they need to learn realistic, meaningful language for that purpose.

Learning and participation

Structuralism and the formation of habits soon came under attack, notably by Chomsky in 1959. Chomsky's linguistic theories are highly complex and perhaps of no immediate value to the foreign language teacher. However, his analysis of sentence constructions and theories of 'generative grammar' with reference to native speakers were based on the acceptance of the creative abilities of language users and the internalisation of grammatical rules. Contrastive linguistics, too, rejected the mindless formation of habits. Instead, foreign languages were systematically analysed according to their phonology, grammar and vocabulary in comparison with English, the native language, to ease the process of learning.

General learning theories arising out of psychology and applied in all spheres of education, not just in language teaching, also moved away from behaviourists' principles to both humanistic and cognitive approaches. Most adult educators, for example, who may be teaching art and craft, history, environmental studies or, indeed, a foreign language, accept fundamental principles arising out of humanistic psychology. Humanistic psychology (Carl Rogers, 1969, for example) is, above all, concerned with the individual, his/her inherent desire and right for self-development, self-esteem and self-fulfilment. Terms such as experiential learning, the self-negotiated syllabus, autonomy, student-centred approaches, and concerns about motivation and individual needs have their roots in humanistic psychology.

The cognitive code, too, recognises the individual learner, his/her desire and ability to think when learning. Cognitivism accepts the physical as well as intellectual involvement of the brain. Teaching practices such as learning by discovery, information gap exercises, translation and vocabulary extension amongst many others reflect the individual's active involvement in the learning process and are very much part of our current educational outlook.

In practical terms those learning a second language need, above all, to be able to speak and understand the new language in the country concerned. They need to be able to understand a wide range of everyday idiomatic expressions, accents and dialects. They need to be able to function in the new language, to obtain and give new information, ask and respond to questions, have a simple conversation with native speakers of that language. Concepts such as social context *will ultimately have to be based, at least partly, on analysis of how people actually talk to each other in everyday settings, such as street, pubs, shops, doctor's surgeries, factories and at home*[6].

The communicative approach

> *Language is a tool used for a purpose. Most people are not interested in the tool as such but only in what can be done with it.*[7]

However, the learning of a foreign or second language would be a futile exercise were it not intended for the purpose of communication. This sensitivity towards individual needs and the awareness of a purpose or function forms the basis of the communicative approach. Its principles, stemming from much work undertaken by the Council of Europe towards a unit-based graded system across the various languages in Europe in the early 1970s, are based on theories of functions and notions developed by, amongst others, van Ek[8] and Wilkins[9].

grammar-based syllabus   **communicative approach**

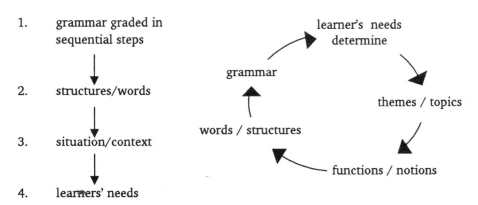

1.   grammar graded in
     sequential steps

2.   structures/words

3.   situation/context

4.   learners' needs

The communicative approach is neither a specific method nor is it based on a single cohesive theory to which language teachers can adhere. Instead, it refers to a set of theoretical assumptions which, in turn, affect the organisation of language learning objectives graded in terms of curriculum and syllabus design. The implications are quite distinctive. Grammar-based non-communicative approaches within, for example, audio-lingual methods, organised language levels in grades of difficulty exclusively on the basis of grammar. The communicative curriculum, while not dismissing grammar, considers above all the learner: what he or she is most likely to have to be able to understand and say in given circumstances, as well as the social and the psychological roles which the learner will be able to play, the settings in which the learner will be able to use the foreign language, and the topics which the learner will be able to deal with in the foreign language[10].

The social context

Social as well as individual needs have, as we have seen, an impact on language teaching methodologies. The learning environment as well as the needs and circumstances of the learners change. Moreover, they are dependent on the economic and political climate of their time. The advancement of technology, television and computer assisted language learning are such examples. The changing needs of a multicultural society in language teaching terms may also force changes in perception, attitudes and pedagogy. The single European market and the increased need for European awareness, emphasis on vocational training and the anticipated impact of National Vocational Qualifications (NVQs) as well as credit accumulation via Open College Networks affect much that is going on in our classrooms and will perhaps change language teaching methods in future.

References

1. Peck, A, *Language teachers at work*, Prentice Hall (1988).

2. Finocchiaro, M and C Brumfit, *The functional-notional approach*, OUP (1983).

3. Stern, H H, *Fundamental concepts of language teaching*, OUP (1983).

4. Skinner, B F, *Verbal behaviour*, Appleton Century-Crofts (1957).

5. Finocchiaro and Brumfit, see (2).

6. Stubbs, M, *Discourse analysis*, Blackwell (1982).

7. McArthur, T, *A foundation course for language teachers*, CUP (1983).

8. van Ek, J A, *Systems development in adult language learning; the threshold level*, Council of Europe (1975).

9. Wilkins, D A, *Notional syllabuses*, OUP (1976).

10. Council of Europe, *Modern languages* 1971-1981, Council of Europe (1981).

Resources	flip chart or board
Objectives	to clarify the relationship between practice and theory with regard to learning theories (behaviourism, humanistic and cognitive approaches)
Activities	Brainstorming find as many examples as possible in the context of everyday life (not restricted to the classroom) of: • behaviourism • humanistic/cognitive approaches reflect, discuss and check that you understand
Time allocated	30 minutes

Resources	a variety of textbooks, some old, some new
Objective	to create awareness of teaching methods and their historical context
Activity	in groups of three or four compare, discuss and decide which teaching methods they reflect. Evaluate their strengths and weaknesses.

Unit 6

The communicative approach

Lore Arthur

This unit looks at the communicative approach in language teaching. What are its aims and objectives? What skills and strategies does the learner need to possess? What is meant by a communicative approach? How does it affect the practice of teaching?

Context and meaning

If language learning theories have taught us anything it is that effective learning will only take place if the learner is actively engaged in the learning process. He/she will be able to use language forms and words more readily outside the classroom if they have been learnt in a meaningful way in the first place; meaningful to the learner that is - not to the teacher.

It is clear that the ability to communicate effectively may mean a variety of things to a variety of people. As a concept the word communication is not particularly precise. Its process, however, requires a purpose and an intention as well as a means and a message. The question arises about what the learner - not the teacher - needs to be able to do to convey and receive messages. What skills, knowledge and competencies are required? What strategies are involved in that process?

Linguistic or grammatical knowledge alone will tell the learner little about social context and relevance or the relationship between those involved in the communication process. After all, everyday informal colloquial language differs considerably from the more formal language used for official purposes. To complicate matters there are numerous nuances and subtleties embedded in human relationships expressed in rich and highly sophisticated forms of language.

Furthermore, language applied in any social context assumes shared knowledge between the speakers. For example, a statement such as '*I am surprised the MCC encourages the reverse sweep*' does not make much sense to anyone unfamiliar with cricket. Both the content and the form depend upon the speaker's appreciation of the situation. As Wilkins[1] points out, the speaker must assess what presuppositions are familiar to the hearer, what knowledge, values, beliefs can be taken for granted.

Strategies and skills

Foreign language learners, then, need to possess not only linguistic competence and appropriate language skills but also a range of subtle strategies for coping in a variety of situations. These will include the ability to cope with unpredictable and unfamiliar language or misunderstood messages as well as the ability to understand which sort of language suits particular settings. In addition they need a degree of social competence, that is a general self-confidence and a desire to interact with others through language, particularly a foreign one[2]. Conversational strategies, too, require the development of creativity and spontaneity, even if the language produced is less than perfect.

Above all, however, the learner needs to be able to understand and speak, read and probably write in the target language. These four skills are often described as **productive skills** (speaking and writing) and **receptive skills** (reading and listening). Sometimes they are also referred to as 'active and passive skills', although 'passive' seems less appropriate since all four skills require the learner's active participation. The language learner's needs will determine which of these skills, if any, has priority over others. Temporary visitors to a foreign country will need, primarily, to understand the foreign language as well as speak it. They are likely to be able to understand far more of both written and spoken language than they will be able to produce themselves.

Model of two-way communication

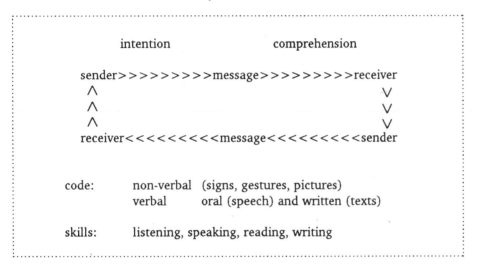

```
            intention            comprehension

   sender>>>>>>>>message>>>>>>>>>receiver
        ∧                              ∨
        ∧                              ∨
        ∧                              ∨
   receiver<<<<<<<<message<<<<<<<<<sender


   code:     non-verbal  (signs, gestures, pictures)
             verbal      oral (speech) and written (texts)

   skills:   listening, speaking, reading, writing
```

There are also learners who need to read foreign texts for academic study or for work purposes. Others may get considerable pleasure from reading literary texts while written skills may be required for certain tasks such as form-filling or letter writing. However, these four skills can rarely be regarded in isolation. For most purposes an **integration of the four skills** is required. We almost always both listen and speak. We may read, speak, write and listen within the same interaction. All of these skills need, therefore, to be practised regularly. None, however, can be learned without discrete language items, that is, specified structures. The learner needs to be able to link these together in a meaningful way. This process requires a degree of knowledge about how language forms are constructed, and how this knowledge can help the learner to speak and understand the new language with confidence and a degree of accuracy.

As we have seen, communicative learning cannot be developed solely on the basis of linguistic knowledge or grammar if skills and strategies needed for communication are to be realised. The simple utterance *je voudrais un*

Themes, topics and situations

café au lait does not, for example, require precise understanding of the conditional. In fact, asking for a cup of coffee can be mastered in the very early stages without too many difficulties. However, the desire for a cup of coffee is invariably embedded in a particular situation and a social context. Required is language expressed in functional terms as well as structures, vocabulary and grammar. It is all of these which the communicative approach to language teaching seeks to address.

While themes and topics are of a general nature, situations are, strictly speaking, unique to the individual. In practice, however, it is the language teacher who, when planning lessons, anticipates situations in which learners are likely to find themselves. It may be outdoors or indoors, while eating and drinking, in the office, cinema or, indeed, the classroom itself. Most textbooks give detailed specifications. However, learners also contribute and create their own themes, topics or situations. These will arise out of interests, experiences and the knowledge learners bring into the classroom situation and which they want to share with the rest of the group.

Furthermore, almost all the language practised is not only applicable to one situation. It can, and will be, transferred to other situations, to other topic areas, in or outside the learning environment. Themes, topics and situations are then useful tools for developing language forms and, in particular, the range of vocabulary in a meaningful context which, in the end, is an essential ingredient in the achievement of sound communication.

Themes, topics and situations do, however, require language in the form of utterances, that is either sentences or words which have to be learnt and practised by the learner. These generally involve the setting of performance-related tasks in conjunction with themes, topics, situations and settings; language functions and notions; language structures or speech acts; vocabulary and grammar.

Functions and notions

The word 'functions' within the current context of the communicative approach refers to the purpose of communication in the new language, that is what the learner has to be able to do in given situations, e.g.:

- introduce someone,
- talk about oneself,
- maintain a simple conversation,
- make enquiries,
- apologise,
- request something,
- express doubt.

These are graded into areas of complexity appropriate to the language level of the learner. Other categories for verbal communication include imparting and seeking factual information, expressing and finding out intellectual, emotional or moral attitudes, getting things done and socialising.

All this can sound quite daunting to the practical language teacher. It needs to be remembered that functions relate, above all, to a language system intended for curriculum planning and textbook design. In practice, language teachers and learners will apply many of these functions on a regular basis without further analysis.

The word 'notions', often used in conjunction with 'functions', may sound similarly confusing. It simply refers to abstract concepts or words which express the relationship between functions. To give an example: the word 'absence' in apologising for absence, or 'aid' in 'requesting aid. According to van Ek[3] most of these are transferable to a wide range of situations and topics (general notions) or they are used generally within specific topic areas (specific notions), while Wilkins[4] subdivides notions such as 'time' into point of time, duration, time relations, that is past, present and future. Furthermore, concepts such as 'frequency', 'sequence' or 'quantity', 'motion', 'space' and 'location' are part of the functional/notional syllabus.

The learner, however, will have little idea about theoretical underpinnings of the functional/notional syllabus. It is what he/she may have to **say** and **understand** that matters. A mastering of meaningful questions, statements and other utterances as part of a dialogue determine the sense of achievement in the learning process. These language structures (also referred to as speech acts, exponents or utterances) need to be practised either in dialogue form, or as responses to questions or messages given in a text. They require the practice of structures, pronunciation, rhythm, stress and intonation as well as fluency and the extension of vocabulary.

Language structures or exponents

However, learners also have different personalities and individual points of views. Some may be more extrovert than others.

> There are numerous ways of responding to a request or command. Imagine someone asking you for some money. You may answer, *'Delighted'*, *'Of course'*, *'Why not?'* or *'How dare you!'* There are cross-cultural differences, too. Native speakers of English tend to be terribly polite and say *'Would you mind letting me have...'* or *'I couldn't possibly have...'*. A non-English speaker might say in the same situation *'Can I have...'* and be considered terribly rude.

In addition, learners have imagination and may want to use language creatively, string sentences together to tell a story or describe an incident. They will need structures, forms and words which will enable them to do precisely that.

The ability to speak with a degree of confidence and ease using a flexible range of language structures is, therefore, not compatible with the learning of a certain set of phrases. These would deny the individuality involved in the learning process. The learner will want - and has the right - to use language which best fits the expression of his/her personality, needs, intentions and opinions.

Speaking and writing in a foreign language also require a degree of knowledge about its components and the internal rules that bind language patterns together. The systematic extension of vocabulary, too, is essential if the learner is to gain confidence and increased mastery of the new language. The word grammar can still provoke a variety of emotive responses. There are some who feel passionately about 'grammar' and others who shy away from it. It is worth remembering that most adult language learners know little about the grammatical forms of their own mother tongue and grammatical terms used can be very bewildering.

Grammar and vocabulary

Yet terms are only words used as 'short cuts' rather like any other jargon in almost all fields of human activity. Grammar presents, at its simplest level, the study of the internal structure of words (morphology) and the study of sentences and word order (syntax). Grammar, therefore, determines the relationship between the various language components of the 'who does what to whom and when' type within a spoken or written communication. The teaching of grammar is, therefore, an integral part of the communicative syllabus. It will matter in practice if the speaker says 'I will come' or 'I may come', if 'something can't be done' or 'couldn't be done'. The correct application of grammatical components such as singulars and plurals, subjects or objects, the relationship of tenses can, indeed, be crucial; they will affect the communicative process and cannot be ignored[5]. The relevance and importance of grammar, however, is determined by what the learner is most likely to want to convey and have to understand rather than what the teacher or the textbook may find most convenient. The learner is, after all, central to all other considerations.

Implications for practice

Clearly the communicative syllabus in itself does not produce communicative competence. It is only through intensive classroom activity that learning can become effective. Most certainly, the communicative approach is no soft option, for both learner and teacher alike. For the teacher it is perhaps harder to implement than traditional approaches. Instead of relying on textbooks and grammar-based methods, the teacher has to adjust, cajole, facilitate, and make sense of a variety of interrelated theoretical approaches, concepts and activities in a learner-centred way so that learners can achieve maximum learning with a minimum effort in the shortest time available.

(See units 8-13 on methods.)

References

1. Brumfit, C, Lunt, H and J Trim (eds), *Second language learning: research problems and perspectives*, CILT (1985).

2. Salter, M V (ed), *Languages for communication:the next stage*, DES in association with CILT (1989).

3. van Ek, J A, *Systems development in adult language learning; the threshold level*, Council of Europe (1975).

4. Wilkins, D A, *Notional syllabuses*, OUP (1976).

5. Widdowson, H G, *Aspects of language teaching*, OUP (1990).

Resources	flip chart and paper, pens
Objectives	to clarify topics, function, notions
Activities	in groups of three or four work out functions/notions, language structures, grammar, vocabulary needed for someone half-way through a beginner's course
Theme, topic, situation	work - an office worker makes arrangements for a work-related trip abroad
Functions / notions	
Language structure	
Grammar	
Vocabulary	
Time allocated	30 minutes

Resources	box cards (two colours)
Objectives	to clarify difference between functions and language structures

Preparation for the course leader	→ Write on one set of cards
	
	functions: i.e. greeting someone
	                 apologising
	                 complimenting someone
	
	→ On another set of cards (different colour) write down matching language structure
	
	i.e. Hello!
	        I am terribly sorry. I did not mean to spill the wine
	        You do look smashing tonight
	
	→ Mix cards thoroughly, distribute one card of each colour among course members who then have to match the pairs
	
	→ Discuss in plenum

Time	20 minutes

Unit 7

Strategies

Lore Arthur

This unit looks at strategies that learners and teachers can employ to make learning more effective, such as coping with different learning styles, mixed abilities, aiding memory, dealing with errors.

Recognising learning styles

Emotions and feelings, referred to as the 'affective domain', clearly influence the individual's learning process. Some learners are by nature worriers and anxious. Others require 'nesting', that is they need to feel secure and comfortable before learning can begin[1]. Furthermore, some learners need group interaction and group support while others are basically happy learning on their own. Paradoxically, the latter will use the group to support their independence. Similarly, there are learners who want a formal, step-by-step approach in the presentation of new language, who need to write down and understand every word cognitively - as most language teachers will know from experience. Yet others appear quite content to let everything 'wash over them'; they seem to learn almost intuitively by ear without bothering much about rules of grammar. Then there are learners who seem particularly gifted, who make progress effortlessly and who may get bored if others take longer. Conversely, there are at times learners within a class who find language learning very difficult, no matter how good the teaching. Yet they often persevere. Sheer effort and hard work will pull them through.

There is another point to consider: not all learners progress all the time. At intermediate or higher levels a degree of 'fossilisation' takes place, where learners do not seem to improve further. This is not uncommon. Subconsciously, their language learning needs are fulfilled. There is no need to progress unless circumstances change. The teacher, then, has to help to maintain and refine language levels achieved rather than work towards unattainable targets. In addition, he/she has to recognise and esteem the individual within a group and, at the same time, actively promote group interaction and sound group dynamics.

Coping with 'mixed abilities'

There are two critical objectives that teachers need to keep firmly in mind: these refer to the development of confidence and autonomy. The learner needs both if he/she wants to use the language independently of the learning situation and the teacher. The learner also needs to feel secure in the knowledge that errors are acceptable, that tension, frustration and anxieties are reduced to an absolute minimum and that speed is not crucial to success. In foreign language teaching, however, nothing is straightforward. A degree of tension can also be stimulating and challenge learners to extend and achieve their maximum[2]. Teaching strategies which challenge and promote learning as part of a communicative approach include the use of:

☐ genuine communication

☐ language related to personal experience

☐ unpredictable language

☐ a wide range of authentic materials

☐ language spoken at natural speed

☐ idiomatic language

☐ task-based and problem-solving activities

☐ target language as the language of instruction

☐ new language forms in context without previous explanation

☐ open-ended questions

Learners will progress at different paces for a variety of complex reasons. Without doubt, however, some will require more time and attention from the teacher than others. A few are simply difficult to teach. Problem-reducing strategies can, therefore, be used to help the 'weaker' learner. These can be applied from time to time, on the spot, adjusted and addressed to the individual or the group as a whole. They include:

☐ chorus work

☐ repetitive drilling

☐ explaining points in English

☐ allowing the learner to answer with either 'yes' or 'no' or to repeat

☐ allowing the learner to remain silent and not to participate

☐ using translation as a means of understanding

All this can be done without the learner, or the group, being aware of what is going on. After all, each individual learner needs to feel and to know that he/she has learnt something. A sense of achievement is one of the most important criteria of success at the end of the lesson for all learners.

Aiding memory

One of the main concerns adult language learners often express relates to 'memory'. They feel they simply can't remember words, sounds or structures from one week to the next and that this is their own fault. Less experienced teachers often reinforce this anxiety by asking *Don't you remember? We did this last week!* We should bear in mind, however, that most of us lead a hectic and, at times, stressful life with many other concerns than foreign language learning. Our brain is overloaded with all sorts of information. Subconsciously we need to select and prioritise what to remember, what to transfer from our short-term memory to our long-term one. Retrieval of particular items is, therefore, not always easy[3].

We remember things for a whole range of complex reasons. Not only the intellect is involved but also emotions, feelings, the physical senses of visuals, sounds, smells, and the feel of substances. There is a difference, too, between knowing about something and experiencing it. You may know a great deal about a country but being there involves all five senses. We remember the sound of the waves, the colours of the flowers, the scents and aromas of the food. In language learning, as in any kind of learning, memory can be aided by the use of sounds, stress and rhythm, colour-coding, gestures, humour, pictures, context and meaning. Words are not learnt in isolation but **in context and in association**. Furthermore, some language forms, by no means all, have to be recycled several times over before the learner is able to transfer them to a new context without the aid! This recycling process, however, will require practice, reinforcement, the constant help of the teacher and/or additional teaching resources to be used outside the classroom.

Strategies

☐ use colour-coding

☐ use specific gestures and mimes

☐ use stress and intonation

☐ use humour

☐ use visuals

☐ provide variety, change

☐ use unexpected language

☐ be selective, not everything is worth remembering

☐ repeat and reinforce whenever possible

The question of errors

All language learners make mistakes for a whole range of complex reasons, be they in speaking, pronunciation, writing or comprehension. How should the teacher respond? Much depends on the initial intention for communication or learning objective described by the teacher or, indeed, the learner. For example, it is perfectly understood within a communication-based context to say 'I go home now' instead of 'I am going home now'. Yet the teacher may have wanted to practise the linguistic form of 'going home' and would therefore want to correct such an error. When and how should he/she correct, interrupt the flow, give the right model? Should the learner be allowed to continue without correction for the sake of encouraging confidence? There are simply no hard and fast rules to be applied[4]. Some errors matter, others don't. There are those which block communication, where the receiver has not understood the message, and there are those which affect the linguistic form rather than the content.

Few errors demand instant correction. The teacher, moreover, should understand that making mistakes or errors is **an integral part of the learning process**. Quite often learners themselves will know that they have made a 'mistake', or a slip of the tongue. Alternatively, learners will know they are getting it wrong without knowing how to get it right. They expect and deserve help. Withholding it, no matter how well intentioned, might seem patronising to the learner.

Krashen[5] in his monitor theory refers to the learner's conscious attempts to correct or 'monitor' errors. He refers to 'overusers', that is those who refer to grammar rules all the time - which can inhibit their performance, and 'underusers' who ignore most rules and rely on their intuition, and therefore often get it wrong. Other theorists compare the learning of a foreign language or second language to the way a child learns its mother tongue. They regard the making of errors as part of the learner's natural progress in the acceptance of the new language. Thus errors will gradually elimite themselves as the learner performance level increases.

Some errors, particularly at the early stages, are clearly due to mother tongue interference. A Continental foreigner learning English might say 'I am in London for ten years'. Other errors relate to the learner's attempt to apply previously learnt rules when not appropriate. They overgeneralise. The learner, having learnt a particular rule may simply apply it when inappropriate. Yet while in both examples the linguistic form is wrong, the communicative message is quite clear. Other errors, however, occur when the learner is trying to be creative in the new language. He/she attempts to say or write more than the language level allows. Should one then penalise eagerness? The answer must surely be no. On the contrary, eager learners will, with progress, often correct themselves.

□ if possible, do not interrupt
    □ give correct model if appropriate
□ allow time
    □ be selective, do not correct all errors
□ depersonalise, take errors away from the individual by addressing them to the whole class

Strategies

Potentially more serious are errors due to bad teaching! Some explanations may have been misunderstood, they may not have made sense to the learner, or involved unfamiliar jargon. Sometimes words explained in the target language only can lead to considerable confusion of which the teacher may not be aware. Errors of this kind can easily lead to anger and frustration - a most serious handicap to making progess. Remember Kidd's commandment which says:

Thou shalt have no universal remedies nor expect miracles![6]

Alas, one also has to accept that some learners are more co-operative than others. Occasionally, there is someone within a group who likes interrupting or seeking attention, who feels he/she knows better than other members of the group or even the teacher; there are also very shy or quiet students who are difficult to draw out. How is one to cope with these? It will be worth recognising and building on the strengths rather than weaknesses of the learner by asking for advice, seeking contributions, giving credit wherever possible in an equal partnership - just as one has to interrupt the loquacious 'know-all' type of student with the 'yes, but' technique so that no one student is allowed to dominate the others.

Other considerations

It may happen, too, though rarely indeed, that some learners express sentiments not appropriate to the learning situation. They may make personal remarks, or racist and/or sexist ones which you as the teacher feel you can't (and should not) tolerate. This is your right as an individual and duty as a tutor. Remember you are not on your own. There are other members in the group, colleagues, heads of departments and support staff to turn to for help and guidance. However, most of the time, course members who may seem difficult at first will 'mellow' and bond with other students in due course. They may have personal problems the tutor is not aware of. Most have aspects of their personality, talents, skills, knowledge and experiences a skilful tutor can use for the benefit of all.

As language teachers we have specific standards and principles, a professional ethos we have the right to adhere to. Perhaps this can be best summed up both from the learners' and the teachers' perspectives in the following way:

co-operation	classroom activities such as pair or group work, role-plays, information gap exercises which promote group interaction, mutual support in and outside the classroom, shared resources and experiences, genuine communication amongst the whole group of learners excluding no one; learning from and through experience (by doing);
autonomy	natural learning with learning often taking place outside the classroom, outside the teacher's control, even when in the classroom; the teacher may create the situation but the learners themselves are responsible for conducting and learning from the interaction[7];
equality	learning involves both the learners and the teachers; it requires an equal partnership with no one being the dominant partner; this includes acceptance of non-racist, non-sexist and any other anti-discriminative attitudes reflected in practices, curricula and teaching materials.

There are, however, other non-linguistic aims of equal importance[8]. These relate to the sheer enjoyment and stimulation which can be gained from any learning experience, the sense of learning not only foreign languages but learning about languages and other cultures. In a multicultural society open-mindedness, empathy and positive attitudes are of particular value.

References

1. Ellis, R, *Understanding second language acquisition*, OUP (1985).

2. Johnstone, R, *Communicative interaction*, CILT (1989).

3. Entwistle, N, 'How students learn: information processing theory', in *Learning about learning*, Open University (1983).

4. Page, B (ed), *What do you mean, it's wrong?*, CILT (1990).

5. Krashen, S D, *Second language acquisition and second language learning*, Pergamon (1981).

6. Kidd, R, *How adults learn*, Association Press (1973).

7. Littlewood, W, *Communicative language teaching*, CUP (1981).

8. Wringe, C A, *The effective teaching of modern languages*, Longman (1989).

Over to you

Resources	OHP, flipchart
Objectives	to work out a set of do's and don't's useful for correcting errors
Example	★ if possible, do not interrupt ★ allow time ★ depersonalise
Activities	work in groups, add more, then one member of each group will join a new group, compare list, discuss, eliminate until you have finite list available to the whole group
Time	45 minutes

Activities	discussion in plenary: examine how your own memory works, things you remember and you forget, what helps you remember things. Reflect and decide how your thoughts and conclusions can be applied in the classroom
Time	30 minutes

Resources	box cards
Objectives	coping with different personalities
Activities	distribute cards among course members, describe on each card a 'diffucult' student. Give reasons, mix cards, redistribute, in pairs work out strategies for coping with such a student, discuss in group, reflect, summarise guidelines for future reference.
Time	60 minutes

Unit 8

Considerations in planning a lesson

Stella Hurd

This unit seeks to draw together those elements that make up a balanced lesson with clear aims and objectives. It addresses questions of emphasis and balance, theme, structure and timing in the planning of individual lessons within overall schemes of work. Suggestions are put forward for classroom techniques which can usefully be employed to implement these objectives, together with some practical examples of flexible materials for different levels and purposes.

Teachers of adults will be well aware of the mixed nature of the average adult group (see unit 1). An analysis of the factors that tend to be a common feature of mixed groups can be of great assistance to the teacher when planning his or her lessons. A conscientious and effective teacher will endeavour to assess their significance in terms of appropriate classroom practice.

The teaching situation

Teachers are by no means a homogeneous group either, particularly when it comes to their roles within the classroom. While some will be obliged to use a particular coursebook and work to a specific goal within a specific time span, others will be at liberty to choose their own course materials and create their own targets for learning outcomes. For some, the assessment task at the end of a given period of time will be the guiding factor in lesson planning; for others, there will be different considerations. Learners may participate in large or small groups, pairs or one-to-one situations, in warm, well equipped, purpose-built classrooms or remote, cold, unresourced church halls. Courses may last a day, a weekend, a week, six weeks, a term or a year.

With so much variation it is essential for the teacher to have clear aims and objectives for each stage of the learning process.

Recognising and assessing relevant factors

Following a coursebook makes the task of defining aims and objectives easier in some respects, harder in others; easier in that the structure is already there as are, to a large extent, the materials; harder in that teachers may have objectives that do not always correspond to those of the course, may consider an alternative structure more suitable to the needs of a particular group of learners, and yet, at the same time, feel constrained by other factors to 'teach the course' as it is presented.

These 'other factors' may include:

★ the desire within a language department for uniformity and continuity of provision, e.g. BBC language courses for all languages wherever possible;

★ economic considerations such as bulk buys, re-sale from year to year, costed loan arrangements for books and tapes;

★ distribution and sharing of resources geared to specific courses;

★ preparation for examinations.

Whether your teaching situation is one over which you have wide or limited control, the starting point should always be the learner. Learners sometimes find it difficult to say exactly what they want out of the course and are often reluctant to express dissatisfaction, preferring to leave the class quietly rather than make a fuss. It is thus up to the teacher to use all available means to interpret and act on any feedback signs in terms of planning lessons.

It is worth emphasising that, while it is essential for the teacher to have a carefully devised lesson plan, this does not mean that he or she should never depart from it if developments during class time indicate that it would be advantageous to do so. Indeed the very confidence a good lesson plan can inspire in the teacher increases the likelihood of such departures being made in the name of appropriate and fast reaction to perceived need. Clarity of purpose and flexibility should not be seen as incompatible.

It is not the purpose of this unit to look in detail at course content or syllabus design; these items are fully explored in unit 14. The focus here is the individual lesson within an overall scheme of work.

In general, **aim** is taken to mean a *statement of intent*, and **objective**, an *anticipated learning outcome*.

The following points need to be considered when drawing up a lesson plan:

★ the communicative functions to be introduced;
★ the language structures to pinpoint and practise;
★ the methods and materials;
★ the order and balance of material and activities;
★ the placing of the lesson within the overall structure of the course;
★ the anticipated learning outcomes.

Examples of aims in a language class might include the following:

Aims

• To promote opportunities for handling past tenses in a variety of situations (intermediate level).

• To provide a range of opportunities for practising language needed for shopping (beginner level).

• To stimulate debate on issues relating to the ecology (advanced level).

Objectives related to the above aims might be outlined as follows:

Objectives

• Students will demonstrate the ability to distinguish between perfect and imperfect tenses through the appropriate use of these tenses in specified situations.

• Students will be able to demonstrate competence in the use of a number of basic structures required in shopping situations.

• Students will be able to cope effectively with the language needed in putting over a point, defending an argument, agreeing and disagreeing, reaching a consensus.

The above examples of aims and objectives give us just the **bare bones** on which to build a lesson and are only a basic part of the lesson plan. Many teachers will want to enlarge on them to state precisely which structures will be employed. What is important is that they focus attention on a particular area or structure, provide a framework and act as a springboard for related activities to take shape.

The average adult class lasts a long time: $1\frac{1}{2}$ or 2 hours in which to cover stipulated material. Certain key questions need to be addressed at this point:

★ What should I include (and leave out) to fulfil my aims and objectives?
★ Which language structures? Which body of vocabulary? Which examples? Why?

★ Which points need particular focus and practice?
★ How should I organise and balance the learning activities to ensure adequate practice in all four language skills?
★ How could I provide opportunities for integrating the skills?
★ Which materials/aids would be most appropriate?
★ How long should each activity last?
★ How will I link the various activities to provide an integrated structure and promote smooth transition: linguistically? thematically? experientially?

Time

The amount of **time** devoted to each activity will vary from class to class. Some activities take off in all kinds of unexpected ways and are worth extending; others fall flat and are best abandoned at the earliest opportunity. However thorough our preparation, there will always be the unforseen. What must be borne in mind is the need to keep moving forward, to cover in that precious weekly slot the body of material outlined in the lesson plan, while constantly adjusting to changes in the span and quality of attention of learners. Many students come to class tired after a day's work, anxious because they have not had time to practise what they learned last lesson, lacking in confidence because (they are convinced) everyone else is more able than they are, but still motivated (otherwise they would not be there). That motivation is one of the teacher's greatest tools in creating interesting and stimulating learning activities.

Students want to enjoy their learning; they also want it to be purposeful and productive. Above all, they do not want to waste time.

Emphasis

The **emphasis** on certain structures, materials and types of activity will be closely related to the knowledge a teacher has of a particular class and the needs of its learners. A language point that is causing difficulty will need to be emphasised in a variety of different ways, perhaps occurring from week to week in different contexts. The method of presentation will also differ in order to provide emphasis without tedious repetition; material on video instead of from a written text; material presented visually on the OHP to tie in with similar material heard on cassette, either earlier in the lesson or in a previous lesson. Sometimes the emphasis will be on particular types of activity which work well in a particular class, e.g. role-play and simulation.

Balance

Balance is closely related to both timing and emphasis. There are a number of stages in the learning of any second language which could be regarded as stumbling blocks and require time, effort and many opportunities for practice if they are to be mastered well enough to be used meaningfully in and out of the classroom. In French, pronouns, reflexive verbs and the subjunctive might come into this category; in German, it might be separable verbs or use of cases; in Japanese, how to quantify or express the subject; in Panjabi, the Gurmukhi script or past tenses.

Each language has its own particular characteristics to which learners will respond in a variety of ways. Individual progression rates will also vary. Whatever the difficulties, learners can only cope with so much of one thing; a repetitive diet is demotivating and counterproductive. The balance of activities needs careful thought, a balance not just of the types of learning activities but of the methods used and the resources called upon.

A balanced lesson should contain the following elements:

- a short engaging opening activity which acts as both revision from the previous lesson and a link with new work;

- discussion of points raised in homework and further practice of materials from the previous week;

- new material;

- a range of activities including pair and/or group work and different technologies to practise new material;

- a lighter activity for relaxation which may or may not be connected with the main body of work;

- ideas for extension and practice at home;

- an absorbing and sustaining final activity to end the lesson on a high note.

    Every lesson should end with the learner being able to see clearly that he can do something which he could not do at the beginning - and that the 'something' is communicatively useful.[1]

Bearing in mind the need to encourage students to become actively involved from the earliest stages, it is essential to give due thought in the planning of the lesson as to how students can best use what they have learned in their own situations, for their own purposes.

Introduction to transfer

    The tutor's role in bringing students to communicate is to make himself or herself less and less necessary.[2]

The idea of different interrelated phases in the learning process which work towards this end is well established. Three separate phases can be clearly identified:

- ★ introduction/presentation;
- ★ practice: pre-communicative activities;
- ★ transfer/independence: communicative activities.

The **introduction/presentation phase** is fully examined in the next unit. Even at this early 'modelling' stage, however, students should be expected to interact by, for example, identifying visual images and learning vocabulary relevant to the communicative task ahead, listening to specific structures on cassette, taking part in short, simple language exchanges with the teacher.

The **pre-communicative phase** offers the opportunity for intensive practice to 'fix' or 'consolidate' specific structures. Activities such as drills, choral repetition and question/answer practice are particularly appropriate at this stage, the aim being *to provide learners with a fluent command of* *the linguistic system, without actually requiring them to use this system for communicative purposes*[3].

For smooth transition it is preferable, where possible, to use the same body of presentation material, pinpointing and enlarging where appropriate. Overlaying transparencies on the OHP is extremely effective at this stage (see classroom activity 1, page 154); so too are grids demonstrating information such as train times, personal descriptions and suchlike, where all learners have the same information and use it for speaking and listening practice[4]. The forms are repeatedly rehearsed but within a controlled framework. This marks an important stage in the process of linking form with meaning and starts to bridge the gap between linguistic and communicative competence (see unit 12).

Towards independence

The final and most ambitious stage involves transferring those linguistic items from the controlled, directed situation to situations in which **real** communication can take place, where attention is focused on meaning rather than linguistic form, where uncertainty and choice are the under-lying features. The student is guided towards the **independent** use of the language introduced in the presentation and practice stages, with the emphasis on fluency and appropriacy. Whereas in the pre-communicative phase the main criterion for success is 'whether the learner produces acceptable language', in the **communicative phase** it is *whether the meaning is conveyed effectively*[5]. This a significant leap for the learner and requires careful guidance through a range of semi-controlled activities to facilitate the development of a genuine autonomy.

It is at this stage that role-plays and games are particularly effective as they present learners with *the opportunity to practise speaking under conditions that are as close as possible to those of normal communication, involving information gap, choice and feedback*[6] (see unit 13).

Working in pairs and groups

The presentation phase is likely to involve working with learners as a whole group with most language exchanges taking place between teacher and learner. The language used is entirely controlled by the teacher and will involve analysis and error correction.

Practice should follow quickly upon presentation. In the pre-communicative phase, pair work is particularly suitable in order to give students plenty of opportunity to familiarise themselves with new language items and gain confidence in using them within a structured framework without feeling 'exposed' or 'put on the spot'. The stimulus for speaking may include grids, symbols or cue cards in the target language; the task will have already been outlined, the language needed isolated. Yet even at this stage it is possible and highly desirable, as students move from dependence on the teacher to being able to communicate without the teacher's help, to introduce a degree of choice within the given framework.

In this way, some of the elements that are present in real communicative exchanges between people can begin to be introduced, thus enabling a smoother progression between 'controlled practice' and 'creative language use' (see classroom activity 2, page 155).

Reporting back is also important in order to give students practice in speaking publicly, albeit in a safe, structured environment where the language has been thoroughly practised. This might take the form of relaying information that a partner has passed on from, for example, choices made from a grid. It might be acting out a guided role-play. Language games involving split sentences or split questions and answers can also work well at this stage, with the class working as a whole group or broken down into smaller groups (see classroom activity 3, page 156).

As stated earlier, it is at the communicative stage that pair and group work can play a very important role in the language learning process. Both provide ideal circumstances for an information gap, an underlying feature of communication: *The information gap between two or more people is fundamental to the idea of real communication. There is not much purpose in asking someone about something you already know.*7

The basic idea in information gap activities is that a common task is set up which can only be achieved through passing on and/or exchanging information. This might take place in pairs or small groups or even whole groups. One or more people need the information you have and you may need information that they have (sometimes referred to as 'two-way' or 'double information' gap). The tasks could involve for pair work: finding places on a map, filling in missing information on a grid, dealing with station announcements; for small groups: coping with directions, checking that information you have is correct, pooling information to solve a problem; for whole groups: matching details, identifying through a process of elimination, finding your partner and many more (see classroom activity 4, page 158).

At higher levels, more open-ended pair and group activities are appropriate, involving such techniques as scriptless role-play and simulation, conducting surveys, holding discussions and debates, prioritising and persuading. Many work well using the technique of individual work followed by pair work in which information is exchanged and maybe evaluated, pairs separating to join new groups with a wider task brief, and a final reconvening of the whole group for reporting back (see classroom activity 5, page 160).

Maximising resources: flexible materials for different levels and purposes

In an under-resourced sector such as adult education, it is all the more essential for materials and equipment to be carefully selected on the basis of durability and flexibility. It is not just cost, however, that should dictate our choice, but also considerations of time and accessibility in terms of how long it will take to plan activities using these materials, how well they will fit into the lesson plan, how appropriate they are for students to work with and how adaptable they are to suit different levels of work.

Visuals on the OHP, flashcards, pictures and objects of all types all fulfil these criteria. They are quick to produce, easy to collect and store and can be used at all levels for a variety of purposes: identifying, describing, spotting mistakes, sequencing, matching. Cut-up texts of varying difficulty are also good examples of flexible materials with wide application.

Authentic texts on a specific theme or topic with linked reading and listening material can also be successfully exploited at different levels.

News items on radio and in the press are ideal examples. A very useful source of these kinds of multi-level activities is *Authentik* and the material produced by the Authentik Language Learning Resources team.[8]

The most important resource is yourself and there is a great deal to be said for teachers meeting regularly to discuss and pool ideas for the use of resources. Resource banks are clearly of great assistance in this respect and properly organised they can save a great deal of preparation time and stimulate a wealth of new ideas.

Post-lesson self-assessment

Many teachers in adult education are now required to complete a record-of-work form after each lesson as part of a monitoring and evaluation system. It is increasingly common, too, for students to be asked to complete a questionnaire or evaluation form about their course. Appraisal and audit are carried out on a regular basis. There is in general a great deal more accountability for teachers than was demanded prior to the 1990s. It has always been necessary for teachers as part of their work to spend time between lessons considering the good and bad points of each individual lesson and working on ways of building on the good and changing the bad. It is perhaps even more essential in today's climate that we should pay due regard to these requirements and include them as a routine part of every lesson plan.

Close attention to all aspects of lesson planning as outlined in this unit encourages clarity of purpose, enables the production of relevant and appropriate learning activities and facilitates the monitoring and evaluation of classroom practice and learning outcomes.

References

1. Morrow, K, 'Principles of communicative methodology', in Johnson, K and K Morrow (eds), *Communication in the classroom*, Longman (1981).

2. Sidwell, D, *Modern language learning*, NIACE (1987).

3. Littlewood, W, *Communicative language teaching*, CUP (1981).

4. Sidwell, see (2).

5. Littlewood, see (3)

6. Scott, R, 'The four skills in communicative language teaching: speaking', in Johnson K, and K Morrow (eds), *Communication in the classroom,* Longman (1981).

7. Langran, J, 'In the classroom', in Sidwell, D (ed), *Teaching languages to adults*, CILT (1984).

8. Little, D, Devitt, S, and D Singleton, *Learning foreign languages from authentic texts: theory and practice,* Authentik/CILT (1989).

1. Draw up a lesson plan to take account of all the stages outlined in the unit, paying particular attention to timing, emphasis and balance. Discuss the format of the lesson plans provided.

2. a. Consider a communicative function that might be included at an early stage of a beginner's course, e.g. buying groceries or stating likes and dislikes. Devise **two** ways of moving from introduction to transfer in the teaching of appropriate language structures through the use of pre-communicative and communicative activities. Be absolutely clear about the materials and technologies you intend to use and the groupings of learners (pair, small group, etc) you would find most appropriate at each stage.

    b. Try the same activity with:

        -   the perfect tense
        -   comparatives and superlatives
        -   pronouns

    c. Teach one of the sets of sequenced activities in (a) to the rest of your group and evaluate afterwards.

3. a. Ask someone to record on video one of your lessons
    b. Draw up a list of checkpoints for self-assessment
    c. Critically appraise the lesson against these checkpoints

4. Consider ways in which an identified body of material could be used at different levels of learning.

5. Devise a series of sequenced activities within a lesson plan that demonstrate the effective use of different groupings: whole group, small group, pair. What factors would determine for you the choice of a particular grouping? What points should be considered when setting up small group or pair work?

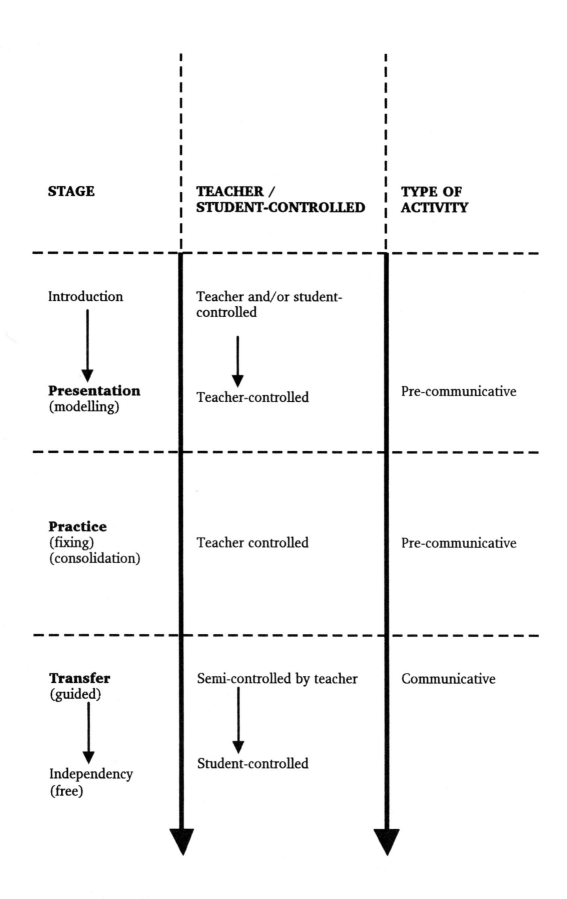

STAGE	TEACHER / STUDENT-CONTROLLED	TYPE OF ACTIVITY
Introduction	Teacher and/or student-controlled	
Presentation (modelling)	Teacher-controlled	Pre-communicative
Practice (fixing) (consolidation)	Teacher controlled	Pre-communicative
Transfer (guided)	Semi-controlled by teacher	Communicative
Independency (free)	Student-controlled	

Sample lesson plans (grids)

Date/Time: 03.12.92
6:15-7:45pm

Course: French for business
Objectives: to consolidate work on numbers/alphabet
to transfer ansaphone messages in L2 to memos in L1
to take part in simple telephone conversation.

Time	Topic/ Function	Activity	Skill	Classroom management	Resources	Post- lesson comments

Class:
Objectives: **Date:**

Time	Activity	Tutor	Group	Resources	Notes

Date: **Time:**

Course (class+level):   **Objectives (short-term):**

Aims (long-term):

Time	Content	Method	Management	Resources
7-7:15	e.g. revision - different content for different phases	'How' (How you are going to do it), e.g. students ask each other or students read, etc	How you would like the class organised, e.g. pair work, group work, teacher-led, etc	Your aids, e.g. book, worksheets, OHP, video, etc
7:15-7:30 etc		BREAK		

(Thanks to Silvia Ballantyne, Goldsmiths' College)

Unit 9

Presenting new language items

Rita Sutton

This unit deals with the challenges involved in the presentation of new language items for learners and teachers and the importance of variety in introducing and presenting such items. It offers some practical suggestions and examples and discusses how to maintain motivation.

Life is too short to learn German.   (Richard Porson 1759-1808)

This amusing thought has in it a grain of truth. The whole process of acquiring skills in a foreign language can be a daunting struggle. The presentation of new material is critical in shaping the learner's attitude towards what is to come and in smoothing the path to its achievement.

The presentation of new language structures, grammatical forms of lexical items is an exciting element for both learners and teachers. For the teacher it is a challenging part of the planning process. Having established the learning objectives of a particular lesson the teacher's next step is to concentrate on the **how**. Where will the focus be? What is the most engaging, stimulating and effective way of introducing and presenting new language items? To think up new ideas, improve and build on others, using a variety of teaching aids for the benefit of the learner can be an immensely enjoyable and satisfying task. For the learner there is the excitement of coming to terms with new material and the satisfaction to be gained from working with more pieces of the 'puzzle', building and extending, making demonstrable progress on the road to linguistic competence.

The method of presentation will often direct what happens next, i.e. how effectively and easily the learner can use the information. It appears on first examination to be essentially teacher-controlled. The tutors, after all, are in control of the procedures; they know the language to be taught better than the learners. The learners, however, are at the centre of the planning and learning process; their needs will be the major guiding factor in both planning and delivery of material. A partnership begins to emerge in which learners recognise the teacher as guide and the teacher takes steps to ensure that learners are actively engaged at each stage. Only in this way can confusion and misinterpretation be avoided and fears allayed.

Techniques to convey new material will involve elements of:

- discovery
- repetition
- information gathering
- questioning
- recapping
- consolidation

In this way, learners can assemble points they already know, a process which boosts confidence and helps to reveal language gaps. By working from the known to the unknown they can discover for themselves the degree of competence they have achieved, which areas still need intensive practice and what else they need to know in order to move forward.

The framework for most language courses is provided by the textbook. This, as we saw in unit 8, will, to some extent, dictate topics and structures. Some teachers use the textbook as a very loose framework, others follow it rigidly, worrying and drilling every point. If it is used flexibly but within a structured framework, it will act as a solid foundation for all stages of work. Many learners feel they need the security of a coursebook to which they can refer. If people are urged to buy a book it should be used. Jumping about or 'dipping in', as some teachers call it, may seem like a good idea to the teacher but learners often find it confusing. It also denies them the opportunity to anticipate what is coming next, which can act as a powerful motivator.

Many imaginative and stimulating ways can be found to guide students into the next stage. The methods the teacher uses to introduce new items will depend on a number of factors:

★ What resources and equipment do I need? What is available?

★ What do I know about my group of learners? Aspirations, characteristics, range of levels?

★ Does the item lend itself to oral/aural/visual activities?

★ If one particular method of presentation has been used a lot and to great effect, is it a good time for a change?

★ Would a change make learners insecure or is it a good idea to bring people out of comfortable security from time to time?

It is important that natural links are made with previously learned material, that each new stage follows on logically from the one before and that there is a coherence and cohesion throughout the whole body of material. There are many ways of dividing up classwork into logical 'chunks' and of subdividing these into cores and pivots around which to link items. The type of course will dictate some of these; others will emerge with time or through questions put by learners. Learners give many useful clues and pointers which can be of great help to the teacher in planning this opening stage of the lesson.

The suggestions which follow can be adjusted to suit most levels of ability. They have as their starting point:

★ a **topic**: introducing and extending vocabulary

★ a **situation**: introducing a range of language structures needed in a specific situation

★ a **structure**: focusing on a specific language structure

Presenting a topic/extending vocabulary: 'the family' (beginners' level)

The purpose will be to enlarge vocabulary about family members and extend the possibilities of conversation about the family. This will therefore be a presentation for beginners. The group will already have come across the use of 'my' and 'he/she/they' forms with the appropriate verb patterns.

Equipment needed: either OHP or board (OHP is better because materials can be prepared in advance and are then readily available to use again, but if only a board is available, then the information has to be put up neatly and as quickly as possible). Giving individual handouts for this presentation is counterproductive as attention needs to be concentrated on shared information so that there is interaction within the group.

Use your own family tree for this. If you do not want to give out this amount of personal detail, then use your 'made up' family tree. This may be necessary if you only have a small family with not many different relationships. Give the group the same option of anonymity.

You should be able to deal with at least twenty relations if not more. This enables learners to have a choice of what they talk about, which at the elementary level is quite unusual. Make an OHP transparency of your family tree or put it onto the board. It will only contain first names and a few symbols thus:

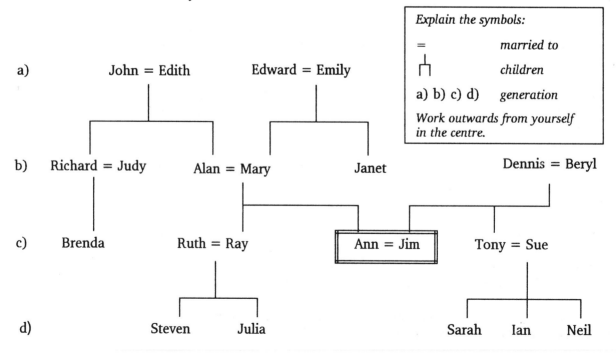

Now begin to tell a story, always remembering to work from yourself, i.e. my name is Ann

> My *husband* is called Jim. My *parents* are called Alan and Mary. They live in Birmingham, I have no *children*. My *parents* have two *children*. My *brother*, Ray, is married. My *sister in law* is called Ruth. They have two *children*. My *nephew*, Steven, is 26. He is single. My *niece* is called Julia. She is 23. She is engaged...

The story can go on. Although individual worksheets of the family tree are not needed, learners can have a checklist of new vocabulary. They can then tick as they hear the relevant family members and write in the equivalent English meanings. They can do this as the presentation story is being told, consulting partners to check meanings. This ensures an active involvement - learner to learner as well as learner to teacher - and means that you can repeat information if people don't hear, thus creating a normal atmosphere with background noise. If too much is done in the classroom in a 'hallowed' silence, it is unrealistic for everyday needs. People get used to saying *pardon?* quite naturally, without feeling foolish. The teacher can control at this stage the amount of information. To check that people are taking in the meanings during the presentation give some unfinished sentences as recaps, e.g. my brother is called ..../ Julia is my .... Students call out the name or relationship.

NB: After thorough drilling of pronunciation and meaning in the pre-communicative period, learners will be keen to 'chat' about families. Make sure that information is given from the *my* point of view, otherwise there will be confusion with some people trying to use other possessive adjectives like 'his'/'her' that they haven't yet come across. The same family tree format can be used to present these at a later stage. Also ask that simple information is exchanged first of all so that the whole process does not degenerate into a one-upmanship exercise where vocabulary is unknown and too complex.

This format can also be used as a known link (with pictures) to describe family members and later still to talk about the past, where someone used to live/go to school/work etc.

This can be a lively and amusing presentation, incorporating mime and exaggeration. Learners have a great sense of achievement because they can understand lots of information from a few cues.

Creating links

Extending language skills is seen by some learners to be fraught with difficulty because they have to take in so much at once, i.e. new vocabulary, structures, themes.

Linking new items to previous knowledge makes good, sound, positive sense. Building on known items gives the learner security, helps the teacher to check and the learner to revise and allows people to lock into patterns and see how different languages are constructed.

This means more than a week by week linking of work. Items learned could be brought back months later to be used as a base or 'stepping stone' to a new section. This also helps learners to bring back together in their own minds how much they can do in the target language.

There are certain useful principles, for example:

- use a known structure to extend vocabulary/topic/situation;

- use known vocabulary/topics to introduce new structures;

- revise and consolidate frequently: check on learning.

A running thread of linked learning could look like this:
(remember this cannot be achieved in one lesson but should be seen as a continuous process.)

→ use **directions** already known to find a certain restaurant on a map
→ use this as a lead into **ordering a meal**
→ use **menus** to revise **numbers and prices**
→ use this information with other menus to tackle **comparisons**
→ bring in realia (bottles, packets etc) and compare, learning **new vocabulary**
→ go back to the menu and describe a meal you **had** some time ago or a meal you **would have if** you had enough money
→ use food vocabulary to start off other sorts of **shopping**
→ then use directions to find different **shops**
→ for each **new** shop think of **known vocabulary** of things you could buy there
→ make up dialogues to buy one of the named items
→ build into these dialogues **descriptions** of size, colour, suitability or unsuitability etc
→ use items selected as base for **talking about celebrations** like **weddings, birthdays etc**

This is only one idea. Your starting point might be other topics, structures or words, e.g. use a **word link 'WATER'** thus

weather forecasts and the future tense
what makes you thirsty, to practise various
forms or clauses with 'when', 'if'
shopping connected with water items
hobbies connected with water
what you did on holiday not involving water
new vocabulary connected with drought,
pollution etc

An example of a situation presentation: 'hotel booking'

The objective will be to explain accommodation requirements. This is suitable for beginners. For short holiday courses and business classes this section can be inserted when and where required. The group will already be familiar with numbers, the date, meals and expressions such as 'Have you... ?' or 'I'd like...'.

Equipment and materials needed: OHP/flash cards/brochures.

Give groups brochures (have lots of these) with information about hotels, guesthouses, prices, etc. Let groups collect words that occur several times, i.e. those that might be useful. Some groups will hazard guesses amongst themselves as to meanings - don't confirm or deny at this stage; in fact give people time to do this exploratory work.

Introduction

Make simple line drawings on OHP transparencies or use large flash cards. (If these have no writing on at all they can be shared by different languages.) Make sure there is no confusion about what each picture is conveying!

Presentation

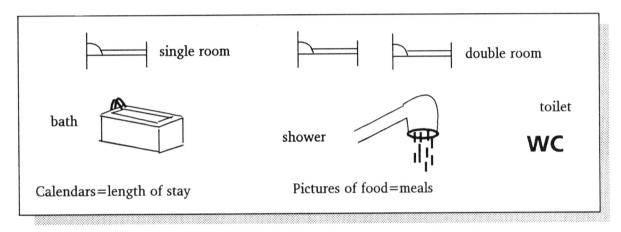

As teacher makes bookings, pictures are shown. Do this in stages:

> *I'd like a single room, I'd like a single room with shower, I'd like a single room with shower for two nights, with breakfast, etc.*

For further examples, including presentation of grammatical structures, see classroom activities.

Maintaining motivation

What draws people to learn a new language? Can any of these reasons be used to keep up steady progress? Initial motivation may relate to having family speaking the foreign language, a desire to travel or work reasons (see unit 1). Some of these will have pleasant associations and social aspects; others will focus on particular needs. Motivations, of course, will change during the course of a session. The learner who joined because he/she wanted to pass an examination may well begin to feel too much pressure and give up. A holiday, another reason for learning, might fall through; a learner who joined for work reasons might be made redundant. In all these cases the original reason disappears and something else has to replace that initial motivation.

However keen the learner may be at the beginning of a course, the first few hours of learning may also cause the first nagging doubts: *Will I be able to say this naturally in an everyday situation? How am I going to remember?* and so on. It is in the early stages of learning that the ability to do things in the new language is absolutely vital if motivation is to be sustained later on. If learners can be shown that the foreign language can be used to deal with topics which concern them, they are likely to be aware of their practical relevance as a means of communication[1].

The learning process is not only different for different people, learning patterns in themselves undergo different cycles or phases in each session. Students will be highly motivated in the beginning of a particular lesson, interest is likely to dip about half way through and usually rises again towards the end. The same may apply to a whole course and to the different levels of a learning programme. Towards the end of the winter, or at intermediate level, for example in the second or third year of a weekly two-hour course, a 'danger time' occurs. This is when students say: *I don't seem to be learning anything* or *I seem to be going backwards*. Learners need to feel they are making progress - even if very slowly. Motivation sometimes disappears, too, as people learn more and there seems to be too much to have to remember.

Familiarity with these learning patterns carries with it important implications for classroom practice and the need to address certain fundamental questions:

★ Has there been discussion about the style and methods to be used?
★ Is the pace right for the group and for the individual in that group?
★ Who determines the amount to be covered in the coursebook?
★ What can be done in addition to the coursebook to vary, stimulate and challenge the learner?
★ How can progress be assessed by the learner?

The teacher's role here is crucial. Working with the familiar while presenting new items can clearly demonstrate that progress is being made and help boost motivation. One simple but effective idea here is to have several presentations in skeletal form to stress **how little** is needed in order to make oneself clear and not how much there is still to learn. Strip away the extras just for a moment and use these short presentations when a fillip is needed.

For example: buying a train ticket. *Single to London! First class return to Leeds*. There is no time for extraneous chatter in this task. Get groups to buy tickets **as fast as possible** until they are doing it almost without thinking. This is also a good opportunity to move around, make a lot of noise in the foreign language and forget inhibitions.

At this critical time, when motivation is slacking, learners should be encouraged to assess what they have already achieved. A useful way to do this quickly is with a series of checklists.

The presentation phase within a lesson is also a time when authentic materials and background resources can enhance the learning atmosphere. If a presentation is interesting and stimulating, even if it introduces some tricky points, the learner has a better chance of working through it effectively and with a sense of satisfaction.

To sum up, a presentation shows what is 'on offer' for the next stage, in which **pre-communicative** and **communicative** tasks will take place.

It should challenge, stimulate and intrigue by its mix of ingredients, both known and unknown, easy and difficult, linking, moving forward and placing before the learner all the necessary 'tools for the job'.

References

1. Widdowson, H G, *Teaching language as communication*, OUP (1978).

Over to you

1. Think of some topics or situations or structures which you could use to make links in learning. Choose one and work out in detail how you would use it.

2. Identify a specific grammatical structure and discuss different ways of presenting it at beginner's level.

3. Are there any areas where forms of presentation of new material and the items/ideas used could be 'pooled' for different languages? How far could things be shared? Is it feasible? Make some lists.

4. If presentation needs to have impact and lengthy explanations are to be avoided, what small items can be useful to the language teacher in setting the scene (given the fact that teachers often have to carry everything in and take it home afterwards.) e.g. a child's doctor's set can do wonders when working on topics of illness or structures of must/may/can....?

Unit 10

Developing receptive skills

Rita Sutton

This unit deals with receptive skills needed in foreign language learning such as reading, listening, viewing for pleasure or for information, using a variety of texts and authentic materials. The aim is to highlight difficulties and develop learning as well as teaching strategies for the benefit of the learner.

'The devil take these people and their language! They can take a dozen monosyllabic words in their jaws, chew them, crunch them, and spit them out and call that speaking', wrote Heinrich Heine (1797-1856) with reference to the English language.

Heinrich Heine was, of course, a foreigner. Countless Britons have no doubt felt the same about trying to understand a foreign language since then. These difficulties should be borne in mind when considering the complex skills required for reading, listening and viewing texts in a foreign language and the optimum learning conditions for acquiring them. Acquiring receptive skills is not a single, isolated process. Learners will receive and express increasingly complex messages which require a whole range of subtle skills and strategies. These skills need to be developed systematically from the first lesson onwards if they are to achieve competence in the target language and be able to use it outside the classroom.

In a real-life situation they will be confronted with a variety of texts and other materials from which to extract specific information. But it should be emphasised that in our own language we also read and listen simply because our curiosity is aroused. We may not have a specific purpose in mind: developing receptive skills may be an end in itself. The foreign language learner will, however, need to build up an inner resources bank, that is, new words and structures which may be used productively later on.

For learning/teaching purposes we need to recognise the important distinction between:

★ reading, listening, viewing for a **purpose** (e.g. seeking information), and

★ reading, listening, viewing for **pleasure** (this may involve the sound of the language, or cultural background information, reading of literature, poetry, newspapers, etc).

Many learners enjoy reading in the foreign language at home. They buy a considerable amount of extra reading material from bookshops or listen to radio/cassettes or watch foreign films in addition to their classroom activities. The teacher should bear in mind the autonomy of the learner when devising activities to promote good reading and listening skills as part of the learning process. He or she will also need to clearly define the different ways in which reading, listening and viewing can be approached and the purpose behind these activities:

★ gist: to understand the overall theme or topic;
★ for detail: to retrieve specific information.

These distinctions will affect lesson planning, the kind of tasks learners are set, the worksheets that are devised, and the questions asked. Reading, listening and even viewing for gist will put the learner on the right track for understanding. Implied is not a vague approach in the classroom but rather a technique to guide the learner, grading the tasks on hand, introducing each step positively. Some learners tend to concentrate on what they **can't** understand rather than on what they **can** understand. As Penny Ur points out:

> *Many foreign language learners run into a psychological problem: they have a kind of compulsion to understand everything, even things that are totally unimportant, and are disturbed, discouraged and even completely thrown off balance if they come across an incomprehensible word.*[1]

Developing listening skills

To understand the learner's initial difficulties with listening, we have first to examine how we listen in our first language, our mother tongue. We often listen while doing something else. Our minds wander: comprehension can be partial, gaps can be filled by our **existing knowledge and experience**. We anticipate, predict and jump to conclusions. Listening to a foreign language, on the other hand, requires distinguishing unfamiliar sounds, picking out words, connecting and sequencing information as well as a great deal of guesswork and inspiration. Furthermore, it requires considerable effort and concentration. The mind dare not wander in case something important is missed. Everything listened to seems of equal importance. Gaps must be filled with our own knowledge of the topic in hand.

> *In real life we listen to find out about other people's ideas and new information. And when we have understood all this, we relate it to our own experience and use it in our own conversation.*[2]

Listening to a cassette, radio, television, loudspeaker announcement or a native speaker on the telephone can produce panic in the learner who may have become accustomed to his or her teacher's reassuring voice. The heard word is elusive: there and then gone. One cannot say 'pardon' for ever! Moreover, *in listening the pace is set by someone else, and the breaks may or may not occur when the listener needs them*[3].

The teacher needs to devise anxiety-reducing strategies to help learners develop good listening skills. Learners should be absolutely clear about the aims and objectives of the task and the way to proceed. They need to be helped to 'tune in' the ear as well as the intellect, if they are to respond effectively and cope quickly, with a subsequent gain in confidence and improvement in speed and accuracy. The teacher should also recognise that concentration spans will be brief, particularly in the early stages, and that if the learner is not understanding very much, disappointment and frustration will set in, which may well interfere with the learning process.

The specific advantages/disadvantages in using different kinds of recorded material need to be carefully evaluated. A well-chosen, interesting recording which is relevant to the needs and experiences of the students will motivate and keep the attention. A text that is too long, badly recorded, or at the wrong level will demoralise and frustrate. Nowadays, commercially produced **cassette** material will involve native speakers and language spoken at natural speed with hesitations, repetitions, different dialogues and accents, as well as the not so welcome background noises. These recordings are ideal for preparing learners for the multitude of ways in which language is actually used in authentic situations.

There is still, unfortunately, a lack of good material for minority languages. Many tutors use their initiative and produce excellent cassette material by recording friends, relatives and visitors from abroad. The **radio** is also of value. It can be topical and offer good variety. However, a radio does not have a rewind button. The language produced is usually very fast and often either too formal or too idiomatic for most learners. From a teacher's point of view there is another difficulty: it can take time to find out what is on where. To compensate for these problems, items such as news programmes can be pre-recorded off the radio, however, and used in sections in cassette form, offering greater flexibility for classroom use. These listening materials are also excellent support materials for learners to use at home. Important points to bear in mind are interesting and relevant content, appropriate level, and opportunities for exploitation.

Like learners, many teachers are nervous when confronted with technology such as a video recorder or a language laboratory. Consideration of the following points can help minimise their anxieties:

★ Is the machine available when wanted?
★ Am I familiar with the various controls?
★ Will there be any disturbance from outside?
★ Will we disturb anyone else?
★ Can the screen be seen/the sound be heard in all parts of the room?
★ What about reflection/dazzle?
★ Is there anyone with hearing/seeing difficulties who needs particular consideration?
★ Is my material relevant and at the right level?

Thorough preparation covering these points will give the teacher confidence and enable him or her to devise appropriate and interesting tasks involving the use of technology. A confident and competent teacher is an essential part of the learning process and in an ideal position to help learners achieve their own personal goals.

Viewing and listening   Many of the points raised previously apply to audio material. Television and video have additional advantages though some learners as well as teachers may have negative attitudes towards them. They think of 'watching telly' as something passive. However, used imaginatively, both can be stimulating, motivating and, above all, highly productive. Furthermore, they offer variety and many challenges. Video work can give another angle to language and topics introduced in the coursebook, and bring them to life. It can enhance, enlarge and extend other classroom activities, provoke curiosity, and encourage learners to ask questions, if not in the foreign language then at least in the mother tongue.

> *A major advantage of television is its adaptability: it is capable of flexible exploitation in a wide variety of situations. ... A news bulletin can provide plenty of meat for advanced learners to study register, to enhance their vocabulary, to do transcriptions, translations, summary work, etc. At the other end of the spectrum, the same bulletin can be used with virtual beginners for activities such as sequencing, spotting anything which indicates they are in a foreign country, for noting any words at all they understand.*[4]

The number of times a section is viewed or listened to will depend on many factors, such as time, ability of the group, the learning objectives, the teacher's preferences, what the work entails, and so on. Generally, it is a good idea to round off this sort of session by viewing the whole item without interruption just for pleasure. The same should apply when first introducing new material. Learners should be allowed to work out as much as they can for themselves, to get the gist of what is to come, before being interrupted by the teacher.

> *Increasingly, we are wanting to base our teaching on 'exemplars' of 'real' situations. Foreign streets, cafés, railway stations, playing fields, offices and houses are the context for language exploitation. Television can come close to capturing the flavour of reality.*[5]

Developing reading skills

We read a great deal, far more than we perhaps realise. We read instructions and/or information on packages, street signs, billboards, advertisements, cash tills, ticket machines, computer read-outs. Most of what we read we discard instantly. Yet we also read letters, memos, newspapers, magazines or books for entirely different reasons. In our modern society we need to read to function, and most of us also want to read, for reading is part of our cultural heritage. There is security in the written word.

In the language learning context learners are, to a considerable extent, in control of their own learning. By reading outside the classroom environment too, they acquire language, new words and structures, often subconsciously, and also reinforce what has been previously learned.

> *When we do not understand something in a foreign language we usually blame it on our lack of vocabulary or of grammar. We feel that if only we knew the words and the structures of the language we could understand anything, but often the real problem lies elsewhere: we simply don't know what is being talked about or what the topic of the article is.*[6]

Developing skills in reading foreign language texts requires different strategies depending on the reader's and the teacher's intentions. These can be grouped into:

* ★ skimming: running one's eyes over a text to get the gist of it;
* ★ scanning: quickly going over a text to find a particular piece of information;
* ★ extensive: reading usually for one's own pleasure, involving global comprehension rather than literal translation;
* ★ intensive: reading of shorter passages, e.g. in a coursebook, to extract specific information, to check accuracy, for translation purposes, summary writing, etc.

Several strategies which aid the development of reading skills can be used. For example:

* ★ placing the headline into a context (e.g. football, politics); we can assume that there is a shared knowledge between the reader and the author of the text, and perhaps a shared interest.
* ★ looking for facts, numbers, statistics, charts, illustrations which help to make sense of the text in question.
* ★ looking for words which are similar to the mother tongue and those which are familiar.
* ★ looking out for negatives such as 'none' or 'not'.
* ★ looking out for adverbs/adjectives which exaggerate or influence meaning, e.g. some, many, too much, frequently, blue, red, small, large, etc.
* ★ understanding how texts are structured; often the main points are given in the first two paragraphs, and at the end. This can be important when scanning for specific detail.
* ★ trying to work out '**who** does **what** to whom, **where** and **when**': creating grids with these headings.

For a teacher it is important to give careful consideration to the creation and selection of tasks to be given to the learner. These may involve among others such activities as picking out key words and phrases, the ordering of information on worksheets, and information gap exercises. It might also be useful to think about the type of questions asked for checking comprehension, that is, the use of **open-ended** or **closed** questions for gist or for detail, rather than the commonly used *O.K.?* or *Did you understand?* Skilful questioning techniques can also provoke the learner into having to actively use new structures learned passively.

There are many things to read:

SIGNS
    MENUS
        ADVERTS
           TELEXES
               LETTERS
                   REPORTS
                      FAXES
                         ARTICLES
                            BOOKS
                               NEWSPAPERS
                                  POETRY

As well as promoting interest in cultural aspects of the country concerned, reading texts provide a wide range of structures and vocabulary on which to build. They can be used for presentation of new language items or for the purpose of revision. Simple practical exercises will serve to develop the confidence of learners and wean them away from the constant search for the dictionary (although helping the learner to use the dictionary effectively should be part of your teaching strategy).

The word 'authentic' can be confusing. Many coursebooks nowadays use authentic texts from newspapers or other sources. Anything 'authentic' should be written by someone else, usually a native speaker, who does not have the foreign language learner in mind when composing the text. Bus tickets, maps from the target country, packets, boxes and bottles are referred to as 'authentic realia'. There is infinite scope for using both authentic texts and realia in the classroom setting.

Exploiting authentic texts

Why?
They form the bridge between formal, tutor-centred classroom activities and real-life experiences: they provide some flavour of the country; they help rapid acquisition of specialist language; they give information about current trends in the country and about the language itself.

When?
As with other aspects of language work, the sooner the learner is exposed to authentic texts, the better, as long as they form part of a guided and achievable learning framework. They will help to develop confidence and enjoyment inside and outside the classroom and extend individual abilities in areas of personal interest.

What type?
The word 'text' in the context of language teaching often refers to both spoken and printed texts. These may be long and complex, such as extracts from newspapers, magazines, books, the radio, or short and accessible items from brochures, letters or postcards. Longer texts should be subdivided. Sections or paragraphs can then be read separately by several students, or given in the form of episodes of a serial. Summaries or quizzes around words can help refresh the memory when the next instalment is given.

Where from?
Commercially prepared material is now available in many languages, though this does not apply to most minority languages. It is much more satisfying and more fun, however, to start your own personal collection. Time and effort spent in doing this is soon rewarded when its effectiveness is demonstrated in the classroom. And remember, most items can be exploited several times over, in a variety of ways and for a variety of learners, from beginners to advanced. Sharing resources with other colleagues can save time, reduce unnecessary duplication and often generates a host of new ideas.

Authentic 'gems' can be obtained from embassies, airlines, banks, companies, travel firms, government agencies, family and friends who live in the country concerned, from other learners who pick up items from museums, exhibitions, post offices, hotels when travelling, and of course from your own visits to the country. It is a good idea to put aside a little time each day for collecting and ... take an extra bag!

Useful ideas and examples

Slides

Objectives:
- ★ to encourage free discussion and develop fluency;
- ★ to create cultural awareness;
- ★ to develop listening comprehension for detail.

1. Find out if the learners have got any slides of the country or of any holiday. If not, provide some. Give individual students or pairs three or four slides to prepare a brief commentary for a travelogue. Follow up with discussion and invite students to write a short piece for a holiday brochure at home. This activity works equally well with postcards.

2. Distribute a sheet of questions and a gapped text to each student, either in the foreign language or mother tongue. Give a short slide lecture. Learners answer the questions and fill in the gaps based on what they hear. They may ask for clarification in the foreign language whenever necessary.

Bingo

Objectives:
- ★ to introduce an element of fun, particularly useful towards the end of a lesson;
- ★ to develop listening comprehension for detail.

After a topic has been exploited and before a video clip is shown, learners make brief lists of words which they predict will be seen or heard. E.g. buying tickets:

- Learner A chooses single/platform/station/cost/how much?
- Learner B chooses single/return/ticket/when/change.

Everyone writes a list. Then the video clip is shown. As words are heard or seen they are crossed off. When one person has found all the words, he or she shouts bingo (or another agreed word) and the video is stopped to check the list. The video then continues so that others can find their words. Then the sequence is watched without interruption. After this learners can get together and make dialogues, using words they can remember or from their lists.

Popular listening activities

Objective: ★ to develop listening comprehension for detail.

1. Learners write down three or four words heard clearly from a selected listening text they have not heard before. In pairs they try to construct sentences using these words.

2. Grids. These are simple to design and can be used for completion by learners when listening to a text.

3. True/false - teacher makes a number of statements based on a listening text.

4. Learners are asked to listen out for specific language items - adjectives/questions/if clauses etc.

5. Combine listening with reading, e.g. maps, lists of dates, price tables, character studies. Learners can be asked to fill in missing information or state whether a statement is true or false.

Objective: ★ to allow students to 'discover' words, themes or grammar points for themselves before being introduced to them by the teacher.

Authentic texts

1. As an introductory activity, collect together a variety of authentic materials around a certain topic. Distribute material among the learners and ask them to spot key items.

    Alternatively, use the same authentic material at the later stages of the lesson as part of consolidation and guided transfer.

2. Give examples of specific language points, e.g.:
    a recipe shows commands:
    - take, mix, chop, etc.
    a set of instructions might show the passive:
    - the unit must be fixed securely before the shelves are put in place, etc.
    an advert will show comparative/superlative adjectives:
    - our product is bigger and better, this brand is the finest on the market, etc.

3. At advanced level use authentic material to raise issues and stimulate discussions and debate.

Objectives: ★ to develop reading skills for gist comprehension;
                   ★ to develop vocabulary.

Authentic material for investigative reading

40
selbstklebende
GESCHENKETIKETTEN
zum Beschriften

| auch für | für | als |
| Weihnachtskugeln | Gläser | Namensschild |

This is from a box of self-adhesive present labels. The season is obvious from the holly. Learners with a little knowledge could pick out words from the label, the meanings of which are easy to guess. The topic could be exploited in several ways for different levels, e.g.:

★ guessing the meaning of other words from the context;
★ finding other contexts for the same words;
★ looking at grammatical points: adjectives, prepositions, nouns, cases, pronunciation;
★ spelling the words;
★ brainstorming for further vocabulary on the same topic;
★ personal accounts.

References

1. Ur, P, *Teaching listening comprehension*, CUP (1984).

2. Jones, L, 'Introduction', in *Ideas: student's book*, CUP (1984).

3. Ur, see (1).

4. Hill, B, *Making the most of video*, CILT (1989).

5. Hill, see (4)

6. Devitt, S, *Authentik: the user's guide*, Authentik (1989).

1. Listening - In many everyday situations people have other 'clues' about what is happening, facial expressions, place. Where should the effort be concentrated then in teaching listening skills? In which situations is listening of paramount importance?

2. Identify a topic and suggest ways of integrating listening/speaking/reading and writing activities at an appropriate level.

3. Can more advanced groups research material and produce simple 'pen pictures' of aspects of the target country that beginners and intermediates could use for reading practice and comprehension?

4. Discuss ways of building up 'banks' of authentic material, looking at different sorts of texts, not only for content but also for structural examples.

5. Can English videos and recordings be used in foreign language teaching, not as an exercise in translating but rather to develop skills in interpreting and to learn how to explain aspects of life in the UK to a foreigner?

6. Discuss different uses for video material. Where is this medium most effective? How much? When? etc.

Unit 11

Developing productive skills

Rita Sutton

This unit evaluates strategies that work to encourage learners to produce effective language skills in both the written and spoken form. These should enable the learner to take the initiative in conversation, to express thoughts and ideas creatively, to ask rather than just respond, to be an active participant in the learning and communication process in and outside the classroom.

When adults say 'learn' a foreign language, what the majority actually mean is **speak** the language. Comments like *'I did some at school but I can't really speak the language'* or *'I can look at a book and know what it means but I can't say anything'* show that learners assess their own ability by how much they can **say**.

> *If students are to learn to speak a language, it is essential that they do precisely that: speak it. That is not easy. It is far easier to learn about a language than it is to perform it.*[1]

Confidence in speaking

The teacher's aim is to produce in learners a feeling of self-assurance in the foreign language and pleasure in expressing their own ideas and opinions, together with an ability to deal with situations as they arise. As well as being able to react and respond, learners need to develop the confidence to take the initiative in language exchanges.

Some learners lack confidence in their mother tongue, and trying to speak a new language will inevitably cause some emotional problems, especially at the start. The emphasis should be on creating a good group dynamic and a **positive attitude** towards learning so that each learner feels valued and able to make a positive contribution.

If learners are given **short-term achievable goals** they are more likely to gain the confidence to extend themselves. Completing a task is very satisfying for both teacher and learner. Staged pair and group work, and homework in small manageable amounts are all particularly appropriate and correspond well to the idea of building, reinforcing and extending, which should be the teacher's guiding principles.

Moving beyond that stage of teacher-led tasks towards a more student-controlled environment increases that shared feeling of achievement and satisfaction, and demonstrates that real progress is being made on the road to independent language use.

Teachers need to think carefully about how best to bring out and utilise the ideas and experiences of learners in devising activities to promote productive skills. In general, context, content and role need to be considered. More specifically, there must be absolute clarity about language learning objectives and methods, and their relevance and purpose. **Clear instructions** about what a task involves are also vital for instilling confidence.

Encouraging learners to use their own experiences in learning activities has two important advantages:

★ it can help to reduce the relative artificiality of the classroom situation;
★ it can enable learners to become more autonomous in their use of language.

Any opportunities that arise for inviting native speakers to participate in classroom activities should be utilised as they have a very valuable role to play. Even learners with very little knowledge can benefit from practising the little bit of language they have. An enjoyable task which can involve all learners is a question and answer session with the native speaker during which the teacher absents him or herself. When the teacher returns the class gives a collective report back on what they have learned about the invited guest. This can be a great confidence booster and marks an important move away from dependency on the teacher.

There will be many opportunities in class time to use the target language as much as possible, such as when giving instructions or asking questions: *'Page 24'*, *'Ready?'*, *'Listen carefully'*, etc, and between learners themselves: *'Can I share your book?'*, *'Do you mind if I open the window?'*, *'I agree'*, *'What did she say?'*. Good learning habits can be developed if learners are encouraged from the earliest stages to interact with each other in the foreign language: *'Are you feeling better today?'*, *'Did you have a good holiday?'*, *'How is your sister Mary?'*

The question of error is closely linked to that of confidence. When/how do we correct? - every time there is inaccuracy? as a collective task at certain stages of the lesson? only when it interferes with communication? (see unit 7). It is important to distinguish the different types of error. Learners tend to see all mistakes as having equal weight and importance, which is clearly not the case. To avoid demoralising learners and sapping their confidence, teachers need to consider carefully their own attitude to error and the strategies they will adopt when learners make mistakes. Pair work sessions offer ideal opportunities for 'diagnosing' any problems. The teacher has a good opportunity to be 'within the group', appearing to listen casually but in fact taking in as much as possible in order to have a 'common mistakes' session later with the whole group. This then does not distract during task work. Homework can also reveal understanding or misinterpretation of work. Encourage even the smallest amount. Once again, common or even individual problems can be dealt with in the group, without any individual being singled out.

It must be stressed that most learners, when asked, say they **want to be corrected**. There is a fine line to be drawn between letting people communicate and build up confidence, and not allowing bad habits to form. Some maintain that mistakes don't matter as long as the general message is put across. This is acceptable up to a point but is rather like saying: *Oh yes, I can recognise that this is a cardigan, so never mind about all the dropped stitches!*

Pronunciation, stress and intonation

Good pronunciation underpins confidence in speaking a foreign language. A frequent chain of events in a real situation is as follows:

The learner attempts to speak in the foreign language ... but mumbles ... or pronounces badly ... the hearer shrugs ... says pardon? ... or worse still, recognising the very anglicised sounds, replies in English! This makes only too clear to the learner that he or she does not in any way **sound** Japanese, French or Greek, and it can be very demotivating.

Right from the start, learners need lots of help and encouragement with pronunciation. As well as doing this in the classroom, they should also be reminded to work on sounds as much as possible between classes. This means thinking about examples and rules given in the lesson and listening to the language either on cassette or radio (see unit 10).

Vocabulary relating to background or cultural knowledge, e.g. place names, famous people, figures from literature or film, even brand names can be effectively used for pronunciation practice. Children's rhymes, songs, tongue twisters are all good sources for pronunciation practice purposes. They linger in the mind, can be recalled relatively easily and usually contain plenty of repetition. Even the most reluctant singer may agree to have a go if there is an evident underlying purpose. Learners can also try to make their own tongue twisters.

How the spoken word comes out can influence how we judge and mentally file away what we think of the speaker and what is said. The same words and phrases can be formal, informal, aggressive, gentle, etc, depending on the stress and intonation and the context in which they are uttered. There are many ways of saying **no**, e.g. anger, disbelief, neutral. Intonation can express emotion, identify questions, point out new information. It gives the language its underlying rhythm: the rise and fall, light and shade.

★ *She dressed and fed the baby./She dressed, and fed the baby.*[2] In this English example the difference is shown by the way the voice is used, falling and pausing slightly where the written form has a comma to show who is dressing or being dressed.

Tone (as opposed to stress and accent) is even more important in a number of languages (e.g. Thai/Cantonese Chinese/Mandarin). It can change the meaning of a word. For such languages far more time has to be built into the lesson to concentrate on this special aspect and as many strategies as possible employed with word patterns, phrases, rhymes, etc to give the learner regular practice.

An example[3] from Mandarin Chinese, which has four tones, is:

Tone	Example	Meaning
High level	ma (1)	mother
High-rising	ma (2)	hemp
Low-falling-rising	ma (3)	horse
High-falling	ma (4)	scold

Many tongue twisters have been devised, based on this feature of the language, such as:

Mama(1) qi ma(3).	Ma(3) man.	Mama(1) ma(4) ma(3).
Mother rides horse.	*Horse slow.*	*Mother scolds horse.*

For most language learners, as we have seen, the priority is to learn to **speak** the language; acquiring writing skills is considered less important for the majority of learners. Nevertheless, it is an unusual classroom in which no writing at all takes place.

Writing for specific purposes

There are different reasons for writing:

★ to reinforce in the written form what has been learned receptively, i.e. jotting down vocabulary, making short explanatory notes, etc. Most learners feel a need to do this and being told not to, because it might inhibit their speaking, can have a frustrating effect on their learning pattern.
★ to consolidate language forms and structures within a given context.
★ to communicate meaning to others via the written word.

An integrated skills approach recognises writing as a language skill which is no less important than reading, listening and speaking.

Learners are going to write, if not with guidance, then on their own, with all the pitfalls that entails. They are going to **want** to write and at times they will **need** to write: messages, letters, notes, faxes, reports. The teacher must respond to these needs, especially but not exclusively within the business sector. Homework tasks are once again very useful for giving this practice. Writing short pieces based on oral work practised in class is a useful consolidation exercise. Two to three sentences are sufficient at first, increasing to a short paragraph as ability grows. Learners can be encouraged to make notes in preparation for later oral work. This may be particularly useful practice for business learners and those preparing for examinations.

Once again, what we ask the learner to do should take the form of small manageable units. Certain exercises and activities used with other skills can be adapted for written work, including information gap-fill exercises.

Dictation conjures up images of school examinations and rote learning. There are, however, numerous lively ways of using dictation to help learners improve their written skills. This can also involve speaking and reading work, e.g.:

★ **dictation sorting**: Teacher reads a list of words or phrases for the student to sort into two or more groups. For example, sorting by tense, function, and so on.

★ **dictation matching**: Student pairs every word or phrase dictated with a list of matching words or phrases. For example, matching comment and response, question and answer, sentence and tag, or matching by rhyme[4].

Learning a different script

Learners of languages with different scripts have special needs, if reading and writing skills are to be acquired. How the teacher tackles this at the start of the course is very important because it sets patterns for the future. Regular time has to be given to looking at the alphabet, building recognition slowly and extending as learners become more confident. Many teachers have established a pattern of setting aside an amount of time in every lesson in the early stages for the revision and repetition of words, symbols and letters which many students find both enjoyable and satisfying.

How long this continues depends on the complexity of the language and how learners cope. There is no reason why this cannot be a regular activity extending into the advanced stages as it acts as a good vocabulary builder at the same time. When learners react with 'Oh not that word again,' they are beginning to feel relaxed, comfortable and confident with the script. As they accomplish more, remind them of how they struggled with what seems to them now a very easy word!

In these special circumstances, going over and over things is not a boring exercise as mastery of the script is a vital part of the process of becoming competent in the language.

It is useful to have large labelled pictures, e.g. shops, fruit, clothing, etc. Put up different pictures in the room so that people can browse at leisure before/during/after the lesson. In this way learners can 'sort' new concepts at their own speed and in their own way.

Flashcards (large) can be used to great effect in the classroom. Make some showing single letters and some with whole words. With beginners, use three or four at the end of each lesson, increasing the number used as skill and confidence grow. Make sure you have several examples of one letter or one word so that although people might work by a process of elimination in the early stages, very soon they are really recognising and not just guessing.

One of the most basic essentials in the learning environment is a writing surface. This acts as a sort of note pad by showing certain models, lists and patterns. The plot or thread of a lesson can be shown on it in note form. This can be used as a check at the end. After a good session of oral work, ideas, conclusions and decisions can be put up for all to see as well as hear. As the speed of the thought process differs from learner to learner, having some form of written information is often important. This can of course be put onto handouts, but concentrating it on a communal surface brings the group together. There is more co-operation. People look up instead of down. Learners can make their own notes and/or handouts can be given out to take home.

Addressing certain basic questions about your own use of a board can help clarify views and stimulate ideas for improved and more imaginative use:

★ **How** do I use it?
★ Does work on the board **progress** with the lesson?
★ Is the board used only as a **note pad**?
★ Is it used to **jog the memory**?
★ Does the board reflect learner's **problems**?
★ Does the work on it **help or confuse**?
★ Does **only the teacher** use it?

Many teachers are confident using an overhead projector. Others are more tentative and perhaps do not get the best use out of it. Informal workshops or meetings through NETWORD (see unit 17) can be invaluable for the exchange of ideas, to discuss methods, possibilities and problems. Making your own transparencies is not difficult with a little help, and many of these can be shared between languages. An easy-to-use guide, *Improve your image*[5] is published in the CILT Pathfinder series. Large, bold, simple 'stick drawings' work very well and give the required visual clues. Andrew Wright's *1000 pictures for teachers to copy*[6] is most useful for this.

Whatever is used, the information must be **bold** and **clear**. It is important to ensure that everyone can see the board/OHP, etc. Is it visible from all parts of the room? Beware of sunlight/reflection/glare/shadow. Notice whether people with glasses or contact lenses have particular difficulty. How well do you know your teaching room? Take time to walk round the empty room and sit in different places. Do this with the light on and off. Look at other rooms, too, just in case your room is changed in an emergency. Be prepared!

Some pro's and con's of different writing surfaces:

★ *Blackboard*: chalk is messy, space limited, details erased, boldness depends on teacher's writing.
★ *Whiteboard*: boldness and space as above, able to colour, able to highlight, whiteness/glare can be stressful, sometimes difficult to clean.
★ *Flipchart*: smaller, less visible, good for small groups, good writing necessary, compact, easy recall so there is a built-in checking system.

Using a board or overhead projector

★ *OHP:*   flat surface needed to project, has speed, information can be retained, can highlight particular points, cover up, overlay; teacher can sit (if desired) and face class, very versatile; good clear materials can be made in advance, easily stored and used over and over again.

Useful ideas and examples

Pronunciation, stress, intonation

Objective: ★ to create an awareness of how to pronounce words in a text, even if the words are not known to the learner.

1. Have a stock of newspapers, magazines, adverts, etc and allow time for browsing and detective work on language patterns and the way letters combine to make words. Encourage students to say words out loud. Give them the correct version.

2. Take some simple words in the foreign language

   e.g.   no/yes/please/who?/excuse me ... etc

   In groups learners try to work out as many different ways as possible of saying each word. Other groups guess (using the mother tongue) the mood or context.

3. Reflect on how, in your own language, stress and intonation play a very important part in the conveying of meaning. Find identical sentences that are capable of conveying different meanings according to stress and intonation patterns:

   ★ Did you see <u>John</u> today?
   ★ Did you see John <u>today</u>?

Writing for a specific purpose

Objectives: ★ to practise writing for specific purposes;
              ★ to develop comprehension and written skills.

1. Integrating skills.

   Choose short authentic texts, either a recording, a telephone message, for example, or an extract from a newspaper or journal, suitable for a variety of activities such as:

   a. learners listen to a telephone message and leave a message in note form to a friend.

   b. learners read a text and prepare short notes for an oral presentation (this can be done with the overhead projector).

   c. learners prepare a number of questions in writing on a chosen topic. They then ask each other in a form of an interview.

They write down answers and then compare with other group members. The teacher will ensure that new vocabulary is shared with the rest of the group.

2. Written information gap.

Distribute to students working in pairs short written pieces that have words or phrases or very short sentences missing. Student A has different words missing from student B. Invite each pair to complete their sheet individually and then compare scripts with his or her partner. This is a useful self-correcting activity allowing learners some independence from the teacher. Pairs can also work on ideas for sheets to give other pairs.

Learning a different script

Objective: ★ learning to read a different script.

1. Letter bingo (suitable for languages based on an alphabet such as Greek and Russian).

    Distribute cards with English letters to match up with foreign language letters on blackboard or OHP, or give out cards with letters from the foreign script for learners to study and then match up with English letters as you call them out.

2. Have pictures of countries, cities, film stars, etc. Put these around the room with labels underneath. Students have four or five cards each with names in the foreign script and they have to match these with the labels and say the names in English and the foreign language.

    As students become more adept, put two labels on the pictures, one for the correct place, person etc and one other, e.g. Venice or Vienna, John Lennon or John Wayne. Learners have to pick out the correct one.

    Taking this further, put up pictures with just the first letters of the name or with letters missed out. Learners have to try and complete each name.

Using the board or OHP

Objectives: ★ to allow learners to take control of their own learning;
            ★ to develop fluency in speaking;
            ★ to revise and consolidate vocabulary/grammar.

1. In intermediate groups, invite learners to have a go at ideas for making OHP transparencies, preferably at home, to illustrate different grammatical points (time and money allowing!). In class, learners form groups, pool their ideas and, using a maximum of two transparencies per group, produce a five-minute lesson. Stick figures, sketches, diagrams, tables could all provide imaginative ideas for putting over a point. It is important to ensure that all interactions take place in the

foreign language. This activity is particularly suitable for classes of mixed levels and gives a great deal of scope for student-controlled learning.

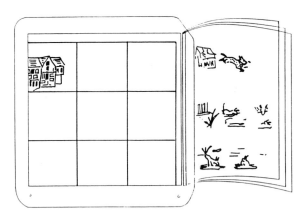

from, *Improve your image*[5]

2. In intermediate and advanced groups, give out children's books in the foreign language. As each book will be different, there will be lots of different ideas for each group.

First of all, let people read the books. They need to be very short and well illustrated. Then either give a checklist of which grammatical/vocabulary points to look out for or let groups find their own examples.

Groups then conduct brief lessons, writing up particular sentences on the board and eliciting from others which point is being highlighted. Class members then make up their own sentences to illustrate this same point. Some will concentrate on verbs, some on adjectives and some on prepositions, clauses or nouns. Each group can decide this for itself.

This is one way of revising rules and noting where people are becoming 'slack' or 'rusty'.

It is refreshing to see learners getting actively involved and chivvying each other along - *You should know it by now! We did this ages ago!*. The teacher is able to take a back seat, allowing the learners to move forward with greater independence and at their own pace.

Many of the above activities will give rise to other ideas. They may have to be adapted to suit various groups and various languages but the basic idea should prove useful.

References

1. Sidwell, D and P Capoore, 'Introduction - the teaching approach', in *Teacher's resource book 1/ Deutsch Heute 1*, Nelson (1984).

2. Crystal, D, 'Section 40' in *The Cambridge encyclopedia of language*, CUP (1987).

3. Crystal, 'Section 29', see (2).

4. Wilberg, P, 'Dictation', in *One to one*, Language Teaching Publications (1987).

5. Tierny, D and F Humphries, *Improve your image - the effective use of the OHP*, CILT (1992).

6. Wright, A, *1000 pictures for teachers to copy*, Collins ELT (1984).

1. Reflect on your own language. Which elements of pronunciation are important and might produce difficulties for the learner?

2. List situations where writing short messages would be appropriate. Devise ways of building on these messages to produce longer pieces of written work.

3. How much time is needed at the start of a course for dealing with a different script? What are the most common reactions of learners to different scripts? Using children's matching games as your guidelines, try to devise activities that reinforce and speed up recognition.

4. Discuss teaching a lesson without any large writing surface and perhaps try this out in the group. How do both teacher and learners get on?

Unit 12

Developing command of the language: aiming for competence

Stella Hurd

This unit will assess the role of grammar in the communicative classroom and examine ways in which learners can be helped to acquire a good vocabulary and become competent in their use of language. The meaning of competence will also be addressed in terms of its application to current modern foreign language teaching and its close link with assessment.

Why grammar?

Stephen Krashen in his work on second language acquisition and second language learning makes a useful distinction between the subconscious process by which we 'acquire' the language and use it for communication and the conscious process of learning which involves *knowing the rules, being aware of them and being able to talk about them*[1]. He dismisses the idea that children 'acquire' while adults can only 'learn', and demonstrates that *acquisition is a very powerful process in the adult*. Language **learning**, he suggests, can act as a useful editor or **monitor** of accuracy, a kind of afterthought for alteration and correction. For Krashen and Terrell, in the method they put forward as the Natural Approach, learning activities should be organised by topic or function and not grammatical structure: *Our claim is that grammar will be effectively acquired if goals are communicative*[2].

In an ideal learning situation this can indeed happen. Adults are just as capable as children of acquiring the grammar of foreign language simply by exposure to it. However, the majority learn in situations that are far from ideal, where exposure is limited and intermittent and time is short. Such learners find explanations and practice in the use of specific grammatical constructions helpful, if not essential to the learning process. Moreover, some adult learners can be quite dogmatic about what they consider to be the correct means of achieving their personal objectives. If this includes requests for 'grammar', teachers must take this factor into account when planning their lessons.

Given these circumstances, while few teachers today would advocate the rote learning of verbs or recitation of drills in abstraction, most are now looking carefully at methodologies that can incorporate grammar in a communicative form and emphasise its important role as an **enabling tool** in the achievement of communicative goals.

*The learning of grammar should be seen in the long term as one of the **means** of acquiring a thorough mastery of the language as a whole, not an end in itself... the emphasis is on successful communication and any learning of grammar takes place only as incidental to this main objective.*[3]

Communication takes many forms and happens at many levels. The language classroom is always going to be an artificial construct, removed from the real world outside; even more so where the language of communication outside is different from that encouraged inside.

Producing the 'product', in other words achieving the task, is extremely difficult, if not impossible, without mastery of the appropriate linguistic forms. It is here that linguistic competence plays its part in the achievement of communicative competence where learners are able to demonstrate a grasp of the relationship between form, meaning and use (see unit 8, page 57: Introduction to transfer). Keith Morrow puts the point very succinctly: *Communicating involves using appropriate forms in appropriate ways, and the use of inappropriate or inaccurate forms militates against communication even when it does not totally prevent it. The acquisition of form is therefore a central part of language learning*[4] (see classroom activities 6 and 7, pages 161-162).

It follows that one of the chief tasks of the teacher in the communicative classroom is to expose learners to a large number of language forms, used in a variety of different structures, combinations and contexts, along with frequent opportunities to practise such forms in controlled and uncontrolled situations. Central to this task is the creation of engaging activities that give a genuine reason for communicating, such as those involving an information or opinion gap (see classroom activity 4, page 158). Learners who have been thoroughly prepared through each stage from introduction to transfer will find such activities enjoyable and well within their capability. They will still make frequent mistakes, many of which could be considered as 'developmental' and likely to disappear without formal correction; the more serious will be diagnosed by the teacher and tackled in a variety of ways (see unit 7). Above all, they will be **using** the language and wanting to 'get it right'.

If we can harness that enthusiasm and involvement by our choice of activity and embrace grammar within it, while recognising at the same time that error is an inevitable part of the learning process, we are more likely to have emerging from our classes students who are proficient, not just at getting the message across, but also of using language with skill, variety and confidence (see classroom activities 8-11, pages 162-165).

Vocabulary may have a special importance for adult learners, since it is the one area of language learning which does not appear to be slowed down by age.[5]

Vocabulary is an area which, like grammar, is focused on by some learners as being a problem, mainly because it is so easily forgotten. This almost certainly occurs where students are expected to learn vocabulary in isolation from any meaningful context.

The acquisition of a good working vocabulary is considered by other learners as the least of their problems in learning a foreign language. After all, there is the dictionary - the indispensable aid to the foreigner abroad. While it is certainly true that reasonably effective communication is possible through the use of a dictionary, the potential for misunderstanding is also very strong. Without some degree of grammatical awareness, the student will not be able to grasp why you can find a word for 'toothpaste' but not for 'could' and is likely to fail to communicate adequately where words with several meanings occur, with a consequent loss of confidence and enjoyment in learning the language. Students need to be shown how to use a dictionary, but, more than that, they need to be given frequent opportunities to participate in language transactions that require them to use vocabulary they have acquired in class, and they also need to be put in situations in which they have a reason to seek out new words.

Extending vocabulary becomes particularly important at higher levels when motivation can sometimes begin to wane as progress becomes less easy to identify. Language games and simulations have a particularly useful role here for both introducing and testing new vocabulary (see unit 13).

Helping learners to learn grammar and vocabulary

The teacher can help, advise and teach, but only the learner can learn[6]. It is particularly important for adult learners who spend so little time in the classroom to develop their own learning strategies, to *manage their learning according to their individual preferences and needs*[7]. This might involve, among other things, looking at individual resources and the appropriate use of them, considering how much time is available and how best to use and manage it, analysing specific language needs and setting realistic short-term goals both inside and outside the classroom.

In the area of grammar, manageable 'chunks' which are accessible and upon which they can build help to reduce the feeling of helplessness and frustration which is common to adult learners. Learners will appreciate guidance with grouping and categorising specific linguistic forms, and suggestions for effective practice between lessons.

For vocabulary, consideration of the following points might be useful:

★ what vocabulary do I need?
★ where can I find it?
★ what kind of strategies might be useful to me in acquiring, remembering and extending vocabulary: categorising under headings? word associations? word games? (see classroom activity 12, page 165)

Extensive reading should be encouraged at all levels. It is also well worth spending a little time with a new group to consider various strategies and to encourage learners to think for themselves and be active in their own learning. The work of Sean Devitt[8] and David Little[9] is an invaluable source of accessible information on current research in this area and ideas for practical application of research findings, particularly through use of *Authentik* - a series of newspapers available in French, German and Spanish with which many teachers will already be familiar.

It is not an easy task to change ingrained learning habits, particularly for those who equate learning with being a passive recipient, even where it can be reasonably demonstrated that it is just those habits that are responsible for lack of success. Only through gentle encouragement and fostering a sense of achievement can we hope to persuade a reluctant learner that what he or she brings to the learning process is of the utmost importance in determining future language success.

'Competence' as a standard criterion for measuring progress and attainment in learners of all kinds is increasingly employed in educational circles. Current interpretations link it very closely with performance. The National Council for Vocational Qualifications defines competence as *the ability to **perform** work activities to the standards required in employment*, while the Further Education Unit sees it as *the possession of sufficient skills, knowledge, appropriate attitudes and experience for successful **performance** in life roles*.

Competence as a criterion for assessment

This link with performance is of crucial importance in the language teaching world and is reflected in the characteristics of current examinations offered by the Royal Society of Arts (RSA) and the Institute of Linguists (IOL), where emphasis is placed on realistic **use** of the language. *The criterion for assessment is whether or not candidates have fulfilled the terms of the task brief in a way that would be appropriate to a real life situation* (IOL). Material is drawn from authentic original sources and each task has a *specific realistic purpose*.

Modern foreign language competence embraces not only the full range of receptive and productive skills but also two other important dimensions of language learning: language awareness and cultural awareness (see units 4 and 5). These are seen to be an inextricable and vital part of the development of skills in modern foreign languages.

The struggle towards a clearer understanding of what is meant by competence and how competencies should be defined has been considerably helped by the work of the Languages Lead Body, which aims to establish a coherent and comprehensive system of skills and levels and competencies through a national languages framework that will link in with the levels set by the National Council for Vocational Qualifications. The framework takes into account existing examinations and their equivalencies across the board. The result will be a greater understanding of what is meant by achievement and progress and a more streamlined and effective system for measuring language success.

The following example of a particular core skill at a specified level demonstrates how the framework will operate:

There are six core skills. Core skill 2 requires the learner to be able to express ideas and facts in spoken forms of the language in a range of situations, adopting and adapting spoken language structures and styles to suit purpose and audience.

At Level 1 (survival), equivalent to RSA Certificate in Business Language Competence (basic) and IOL Preliminary, the candidate must demonstrate competence in the following areas:

Key competence   Copes with simple practical needs in a social or work setting. Is able to survive in straightforward and familiar situations.

Language usage   Uses a limited range of language, mostly memorised but with some simple variants. Has a partial knowledge of basic structures. Commands enough language to cope with the most common everyday needs.

Types of language tasks   Can exchange basic information. Can complete basic transactions of a simple, practical nature. Can deliver short memorised or prompted talks. Can offer simple explanations. Can establish and maintain simple social relationships. Can converse at a simple level on the most common topics. Can initiate as well as respond in basic exchanges.

Quality of language use   Discourse lacks fluency and is frequently hesitant or unclear. Accuracy is sufficient to convey basic information. Pronunciation and intonation are intelligible to a sympathetic native listener.

Quality of communication   Conversation frequently breaks down, although command of language strategies is sufficient to persist until communication has been effected, with support from the listener. Frequently needs repetition and paraphrase in order to take part in exchanges.

Implications for classroom practice

Whether or not we are preparing students for examinations, we need, as teachers, to create activities that lead to carefully devised learning outcomes, relevant to the needs of students and capable of modification and extension where need dictates.

As assessment is seen more and more to be an integral part of language learning, it becomes equally important to relate these activities and learning outcomes to a range of competencies defined internally or by external agencies. Such efforts bring their own reward. Demonstration of language proficiency is allowed to act both as a motivational force and a monitor of progress for both learner and teacher, course design is simplified and more finely tuned, and the process of learning a language is demystified and made accessible to an ever increasing range of language learners. In short, we are able to offer learners the opportunity to achieve what it is they claim to want: sufficient competence in the language to understand and be understood through a variety of communicative channels and in a variety of situations.

References

1. Krashen, S D, *Principles and practice in second language acquisition*, Pergamon (1982).

2. Krashen, S D and T D Terrell, *The natural approach: language acquisition in the classroom*, Pergamon/Alemany (1983).

3. Ur, P, *Grammar practice activities*, CUP (1988).

4. Morrow, K, 'Principles of communicative methodology', in Johnson, K and K Morrow (eds), *Communication in the classroom*, Longman (1981).

5. Rivers, W M, *Communicating naturally in a second language*, CUP (1983). Cited by Taylor, L, *Teaching and learning vocabulary*, Prentice Hall (1990).

6. Morrow, see (4).

7. Ellis, G and B Sinclair, *Learning to learn English*, CUP (1989).

8. Devitt, S, *Authentik: the user's guide*, Authentik (1991).

9. Little, D, *Self-access systems for language learning*, Authentik/CILT (1989).

Additional useful sources

Littlewood, W, *Communicative language teaching*, CUP (1981).

Littlewood, W, *Foreign and second language learning*, CUP (1984).

Sidwell, D (ed), *Teaching languages to adults*, CILT (1984).

Sidwell, D, *Modern language learning*, NIACE (1987).

Wilkins, D A, *Linguistics in language teaching*, Edward Arnold (1972).

1.   Choose one of the activities in the classroom activities section and work out ways in which it could be adapted or modified to suit the language needs of your particular class.

2.   The following list gives ideas on the types of activities that could be used to practise and extend vocabulary. Choose **three** and advise on ways in which they could be exploited for any language class, paying particular attention to timing, follow-up and placing within the structure of the lesson:

      synonyms and antonyms
      true/false statements
      grids
      crosswords
      word clusters
      brainstorming
      split questions/answers, statements, headlines (see classroom activity 3, page 156)
      prioritising
      wordsearches
      nonsense texts
      word chains and associations
      re-translation

3.   Start compiling and filing under appropriate headings activities that you intend to use or have already used.

4.   What would you consider is meant by the word 'competence' in language learning? Draw up five competencies that you consider an essential part of a beginners' course during the first term.

Unit 13

Additional materials & alternative methods

Stella Hurd

This unit introduces and evaluates a range of additional materials that can be integrated into lessons to provide variety, increase the input of authentic language, and aid in the acquisition and development of receptive and productive skills. It also examines a lesser known teaching method which, through its emphasis on relaxation and independence, has elements that correspond well to the requirements of a learner-centred approach.

For teachers of English, French, German and, to some extent, Spanish and Italian, the need for supplementary materials might well be questioned. There are so many excellent coursebooks available with linked cassette and video material, why should it be necessary to embark on the time-consuming activity of making, collecting and devising appropriate ways of using extra materials?

Why use supplementary materials?

For those at the other extreme, teaching languages that attract fewer students, such as Welsh, Chinese, Arabic or Gujerati, there is a very evident need for additional course materials. The few published materials available are often inappropriate for adult learners, old-fashioned, dull or ill-suited to the demands of a modern communicative classroom. The teacher is, in effect, forced to look further afield for stimulating and relevant materials.

Yet even if there is a wide variety of coursebooks, cassettes, videos and workbooks available in your particular language, there are still many reasons why supplementary materials should be allowed to enhance the learning experience. Used appropriately they can:

- encourage independence in both teacher and learner;
- increase motivation through relating to and utilising students' own experience;
- provide enjoyable opportunities for revision, recap and feedback;
- aid the acquisition of vocabulary and structure through reinforcement;
- extend and update knowledge about the country, its people, customs and language;
- boost confidence in less able learners;

- enliven a dull coursebook presentation;
- engage and involve learners whose needs are the guiding factor in the choices that teachers make, and who may themselves also have been instrumental in the collecting and selecting of such materials;
- introduce aspects of language learning that are absent from the material available, e.g. paralinguistic elements: gesture, facial expression, intonation, register and nuance;
- give a different angle on a language point that is proving difficult to grasp and use with communicative competence.

Different materials: different technologies

A teacher standing before the class day after day, week after week, year after year, needs every support if s/he is not to be drained of initiative, the ability to create dramatic impacts and to successfully manage the complex learning patterns of different students.[1]

Categorising supplementary materials under different headings can help provide the teacher with a useful overview of what is available and give some pointers as to how, when and for what purpose particular items might best be used. Such headings would include:

Realia: bus tickets, foreign currency, menus, bottles, packets, ... These have a particularly useful function in the classroom, that of increasing the desirable authenticity *while reducing the inevitable artificiality of the teaching/learning situation*[2].

Authentic reading materials: newspapers, magazines, brochures, notices ... (see unit 10)

Authentic listening and viewing materials: conversations, news bulletins, debates, discussions, weather forecasts, extracts from TV and radio programmes ...(see units 10 and 11)

OHP transparencies: (see unit 11 and classroom activity 1, page 154)

Language games and activities: (see this unit and classroom activities: in particular 3, 4, 6, 7, 8, 10 & 11, pages 156-165)

Songs, poems, plays and literary extracts: (see this unit)

Worksheets, grids and puzzles: (see classroom activities 9, page 163, & 12, page 165)

Computer software: (see unit 15)

Using language games

Games can be found to give practice in all the skills (reading, writing, listening and speaking), in all stages of the teaching/learning sequence (presentation, repetition, recombination and free use of language) and for many types of communication (e.g. encouraging, criticising, agreeing, explaining).[3]

The flood of books on language games and activities onto the market in the 1980s was ample proof of their wide acceptance in the world of language teaching. It would be true to say that they are now considered as central to many a language programme and that the idea of games as a purely marginal activity is virtually obsolete. Their appeal lies in the opportunity they provide for spontaneous authentic language practice *without the controlling influence of the teacher or the course book*[4] and in the simple fact that they are highly enjoyable. Games can be of great value at that important stage described in unit 8 which marks the **transition from introduction to transfer**, lying as they do somewhere between *the controlled context of the formal lesson and the real-life situation outside the classroom*[5]. Pre-communicatively they can be used to practise a specific linguistic form (see classroom activities 6-8, pages 161-162), but their real value lies in the fact that they give learners a **genuine reason to want to speak**, and thus correspond very well to the requirements of a learner-centred communicative methodology (see classroom activity 4, page 158). The more absorbing the game, the more urgent the need to communicate and, consequently, the greater the amount of language generated.

> *It has been shown that the average teacher in Europe today notches up a score of about 60-70% teacher-talking time in his or her classes. Just 35% is left to the students.*[6]

The fact that the game-playing situation is in a sense artificial has certain psychological advantages in that learners do not have to worry about the consequences of inaccuracy or misunderstanding in the same way as they might in the 'real world', and are therefore more likely to take risks and 'try out' language constructions. The achievement of successful communication in these circumstances can act as a great confidence booster. For the teacher - freed from centre stage to circulate, act as a resource if required, note common areas of difficulty, participate if appropriate - games can serve as a useful 'diagnostic tool'[7], a means of checking on learning in a non-intrusive manner and taking appropriate remedial action as and when required.

Role-play and simulation

All that is said about games can apply equally well to role-play and simulation. Both, like all language games, are excellent methods of introducing variety and reality to the classroom and of extending social interaction beyond the confines of the coursebook.

Role-play

Role-play is a particularly flexible classroom technique in that it can be employed equally well at all stages from presentation through practice to free communication and therefore provides continuity in bridging the gap between form and function.

It is an integral feature of many examinations, including those offered by the RSA, Institute of Linguists and Cambridge Local Examinations Syndicate where scripted dialogues, prompt cues and unscripted task outlines all play their part.

Increasingly, role-play is used as part of a chain of integrated activities. Learners might be asked to extract information from written material, then to use or add to that information using role-play, and finally to relay all the information gathered to a third party in written form. In this way the four language skills - reading and listening (receptive) and speaking and writing (productive) - are integrated into one activity which is of a practical nature, relevant to the needs of most adult learners.

The following examples demonstrate the effectiveness of role-play for both linguistic and communicative purposes (see also classroom activities 2, 4, 9 and 11 in unit 19).

GENERAL CERTIFICATE   ORAL TASK   ITALIAN
(Institute of Linguists, 1990)

Task-based activity (for communicative purposes)
Candidate's task brief

You are in San Marino with your family and are thinking of visiting Rimini on Saturday. You notice that an Italian visitor at your hotel (the examiner) has a time-table and you ask him about services.

You open the conversation by greeting the Italian visitor and introducing yourself. Explain what your plans are and find out what kind of time-table the visitor has.

Ask about:
- Saturday availability
- departure time
- the time of the return journey
- the cost
- the departure point in San Marino

Make note of:
- the departure time from San Marino and the departure time from Rimini_____

  _____

- the departure point in San Marino_____

  _____

Scripted dialogue *(for linguistic purposes: to practise past tenses)*

A: Did you go out last night?
B: Yes, I went to the cinema with Suzanne and Fred.
A: What did you see?
B: It was a film called 'Images of youth'.
A: What was it about?
B: Three soldiers who met up again 30 years after the war and re-lived their lives through flashback.
A: Was it sad?
B: Yes, a little. In fact Suzanne was crying at the end.
A: Did you go home straight afterwards, because I phoned you about 11p.m. and there was no reply?
B: No, I went to Suzanne's for a coffee. It was freezing cold and I didn't even have a coat. I got back about midnight and then went straight to bed.
A: Are you doing anything tonight?
B: No, I think I'll stay in.
A: Me too.
B: See you Friday then.
A: Yes, bye.

As learners progress through a range of role-plays, becoming increasingly independent in their language output, teacher control is gradually relaxed, and 'creative' language use is encouraged and expected. It is important to bear in mind, however, that although language output becomes less and less controlled, the teacher is still 'in charge' in that it is up to him or her to decide when to move on to each stage of the learning process, when to pause for a collective feedback session, when to re-introduce more controlled activities to practise language forms that have clearly not been mastered. Role-play can provide many useful diagnostic clues for the teacher and help organise future lesson planning.

Simulation properly belongs in the group of communication activities where interaction is not controlled, students 'inhabit' a role but are themselves at all times. It is a challenging and demanding activity, suited best to learners at higher levels. A simulation can last 15 minutes or several hours - an important factor to bear in mind. The emphasis is on such functional skills as eliciting, persuading, dissuading, agreeing, disagreeing, criticising and defending a point. There will usually be a certain amount of information to assimilate before the simulation can begin, and other information which will emerge once it has started. In this way the skills of reading, listening and speaking can be usefully integrated in a natural, uncontrolled way. Students can really say what they think and have a lot of fun in their attempts to air their views and make their feelings known. The following simulation from the *France extra guide for teachers* is one of several good examples to be found in the guide. It is simple to set up, enjoyable for all participants and could be easily adapted for other languages:

Simulation

Le Salon du Prêt-à-Porter

The students will be either boutique owners or sales reps. Each rep will be trying to persuade the boutique owners to stock their goods in the next financial year. They will be armed with one of the fashion magazines which will represent their collection and each will have a different magazine and therefore a different 'collection'. Each boutique is run by two people who have to discuss with the sales rep in turn the merits of various garments and decide which to take, and how many. They have a budget of around 100 000 Francs.

There should be the same number of reps as boutiques, i.e. twice as many owners as reps, so that as the reps examine each 'stand', armed with either *Elle, Cosmo, Marie-Claire* or *Femme*, everyone will be engaged in negotiation at the same time, at least at the beginning. It is interesting to compare each boutique's 'collection' at the end.[8]

Drama and improvisation

Drama and improvisation could be seen as going one stage further on the road towards creative, independent language use, as the *form of role-playing in which learners can be most creative, because they are most able to act out personal interpretations of the situation and their roles within it*[9]. As well as giving learners the opportunity to use and experiment with language, drama and improvisation techniques draw attention, like video, to the importance of paralinguistic factors in communication: gesture, expression, body language. Other external features such as clothing and general appearance take on a new significance and are seen, too, to have an influence on the way we communicate.

The key element in drama and improvisation is **imagination** which can be a great motivating factor. Learners are free to portray characters of their own making, to *explore and exploit their communicative repertoire in any ways they wish*[10].

Adult learners of an extrovert nature will often excel at this kind of activity and be instrumental in contributing to a general atmosphere of fun and relaxation. On the other hand, shy or slow learners may be unwilling or unable to participate. Some profess quite openly to have 'no imagination' and find the whole idea of taking on a role and expressing opinions bewildering and painful. They feel inhibited by the performance of others and are thus likely to have negative feelings about themselves reinforced.

There are others who find this type of activity without value and a waste of time, precisely because it is not controlled. It is important to find ways of enabling all learners to fully realise their potential, while at the same time ensuring that feelings are respected and dignity left intact.

Drama and improvisation, role-play and simulation are ideal techniques for releasing inhibitions that can act as barriers to learning. They also help establish a co-operative, collaborative atmosphere which enables learners to learn a great deal about themselves and others through collective interaction, to engage at their own level in their own chosen manner, to surprise and be surprised, and to discover their own personal language 'gaps'. They are not just techniques, but embody an important educational philosophy - that learners are autonomous human beings capable of taking charge of events and making decisions, and above all of being *active participants in the learning process*[11].

It should be remembered that *the emphasis in these activities is on practising the **process** of communicating rather than on evaluating its **product***[12]. Nevertheless, free, uncontrolled activities can pose problems of management and intervention for the teacher. To minimise these it is helpful to pay particular attention to the following points:

★ relevance to a group with very diverse needs and abilities
★ usefulness where class contact time is severely limited
★ psychological factors
★ method and timing of de-briefing, error analysis and correction

Songs, poems and literary extracts

For many adult learners and teachers the introduction of a song or poem into the lesson has little appeal. In the case of a song, lack of musical ability on the part of the teacher or negative feedback from students may well act as a strong deterrent when lessons are being planned. A poem might seem too abstract, involve too much unknown vocabulary or structure, or simply seem inappropriate to a particular group of learners. The same might apply to a literary text.

It would, however, be unwise to ignore the cultural significance of this kind of material and the wealth of possibilities it can open up to willing learners for follow-up work which is both stimulating and enjoyable. A song, for example, can be used to introduce a theme, as a starting point for discussion or as a follow-up or an introduction to poetry. *It is an ideal teaching unit, lasting approximately three minutes, filling less than a side of paper, containing repetition of basic vocabulary and key phrases, and frequently touching profound and controversial philosophy. Add to this the great variety of music, and what more could you want?*[13] For those for whom this kind of activity has appeal there is a vast repertoire from which to choose in virtually every language. Many songs and poems give ideal opportunities, too, for reinforcement and practice of specific linguistic forms.

Inventing or adapting words in the target language to well-known tunes can also be very effective, e.g. parts of the body to the tune of *There is a tavern in town*.

For listening comprehension, there are many activities that have been shown to work well:

★ gapped texts: not too many gaps ... suitable for short songs. Students might also be asked to take home the text and guess the missing words in preparation for a collective class effort next session.

★ aural comprehension exercises: pre-questions can be set to guide the listening.

★ grids: for noting specific information.

★ lists of words: ticking off words as they are heard.

★ rhyming words: giving a word that occurs at the end of a line, playing the tape and pausing for students to guess the word that rhymes with it. In French the word *dos* (back) might give *faux, beau, eau/au, mot/maux, nos, pot/peau, sot/sceau, taux/tôt, trop, chaud, veau/vos* and possibly many others. Exploring the possibilities can be both enjoyable and valuable.

Literary extracts are often introduced in response to student demand for some continuous prose which is at an appropriate level. The adult language learner in the once-weekly class at around intermediate level often expresses a wish to stretch beyond the situational dialogues which have formed the bulk of the learning programme, but does not yet feel ready for a full-scale novel. Carefully chosen, a literary extract can provide much enjoyment and induce a sense of real achievement. Short stories are ideal as they can be covered in one session, though there are certain advantages in tackling a larger extract and breaking off at a dramatic point in the story to maintain interest from week to week. While ideas for exploitation could include the range of activities commonly adopted for use with reading texts in class, such as oral comprehension questions, retranslation of selected phrases or true/false statements, the primary aim in integrating such literary texts into the language class is to encourage the pleasurable aspect of reading for its own sake, focusing on the added dimension it can bring to the learning process; in the same way, many learners find the interrelation of music and poetry a particularly pleasurable and satisfying experience.

Two enjoyable and productive activities worth a mention which combine reading, oral and aural skills are, firstly, 'jigsaw' reading with reporting back (see classroom activity 5, page 160); secondly, inviting students to participate in the story, either by predicting in groups what might come next, or by acting out a role-play based on the story line. This latter activity has also proved successful with extracts from films or television programmes where the learner is invited to interact, rather than remain a passive recipient.

One alternative approach: *Suggestopedia*

Suggestopedia is the name given to a teaching method devised by a Bulgarian psychotherapist, Georgi Lozanov, in the early 1970s. Lozanov's observations on learning, based on controlled experiments, were that learning ability is far superior than commonly assumed, that learning involves the entire person and that there are many 'anti-suggestive' barriers in people which may interfere with the learning process. Suggestopedia aims to break down these barriers by *relaxing the student, reducing anxieties, removing mental blocks and building confidence*[14].

Its four underlying principles are:

★ the use of peripheral perception which is linked to long-term memory;
★ the use of information that is personalised;
★ assimilation before analysis;
★ the right to make mistakes.

The suggestopedic course

A suggestopedic course is divided into units which contain texts of dialogues in the target language, presented in short lines with a mother tongue translation at the side. The texts which are designed *not only to be of inherent interest but also to be of some practical value and relevant to the student's need*[15], together with activities for exploitation, generally take up five three-hour periods in a week. Courses usually last four or five weeks.

Each student is given a new identity to provide a *mask or shield behind which he is safe to develop as he likes, and to make mistakes without personal jeopardy*[16].

A typical first week might run as follows[17]:

MONDAY	TUESDAY	WEDNESDAY	THURSDAY	FRIDAY
First day entry exams to determine levels.	Activation phase of Lesson 1.	Adaptation phase of Lesson 1. An easy test (lasts five minutes).	Activation phase of Lesson 2.	Adaptation phase of Lesson 2. An easy test.
BREAK	BREAK	BREAK	BREAK	BREAK
Role distribution. Presentation concert to classical music of Lesson 1. Decoding session. Light music.	Activation phase (one hour). Relaxation concert (1/2 hour).	Presentation classical concert of Lesson 2. Decoding session. Light music.	Activation phase (one hour). Relaxation concert of Lesson 2 (1/2 hour).	Presentation classical concert of Lesson 3. Decoding session. Light music.

The active concert, so called because students 'actively follow', describes the presentation of the text to classical music. The teacher reads in sympathy with the music - high, medium or low - *giving emphasis by pauses, allowing phrases to echo in the memory*[18], closely following rhythm and dynamics to produce an impression of harmonious blending.

The passive concert differs in a number of ways: lights are dimmed, students sit comfortably with eyes closed and listen while the text is read again, this time to Baroque music. *Listening to Baroque music the body is relaxed, the brain is alert, receiving information without* **'conscious effort'**[19] (our emphasis).

The active and passive concerts

The activation phase takes the form of a *quick succession of activities and games that are fast-moving, fun, varied, stimulating and gratifying, where the emphasis is on communication rather than language*[20]. They are firmly based on the text and designed to exploit the language it contains as closely as possible.

The activation and adaptation phases

The adaptation phase opens up the possibility for language learned to be used in less controlled contexts. It is similar to the 'free end' of the controlled ↔ uncontrolled language continuum which forms the basic structure of communicative methodology. The activities are again *quick-moving, fun and communication-oriented*[21], involving the use of games, a range of authentic materials, and often mini-plays or skits.

Adherents to the suggestopedic method will point to the number of students demonstrating an acceptable level of linguistic competence and increased self-confidence after participating in a course. It is without doubt a method that embraces many of the priorities of current teaching methodology, for example: active learning in a pleasant, stress-free environment, communicative techniques, a co-operative spirit, positive reinforcement. Nor does it shy away from the more formal elements of language learning such as grammar and testing. Grammar is slotted in at intervals, more as a post-script than a pre-communicative linguistic tool. *All the grammar being explained is grammar of which the students already have an intuitive and spontaneous grasp*[22].

How effectively do students learn?

One and a half hour tests take place at the beginning of every training session to measure objective levels, and at the end, to measure progress. In addition, mini-tests lasting five to ten minutes are often set at intervals throughout the course. They are designed to *constitute credible reinforcement of what has been learned... and aim at showing students how much they know*[23].

Suggestopedia is unlikely to have universal appeal. Crucial factors determining successful outcomes will be the **attitudes and personalities** of both teacher and learner. A suggestopedic teacher must be highly skilled, have a very dynamic personality and possess enormous reserves of energy. The learner must be really willing to let go and to play an active role. There are undoubtedly many adult teachers and learners who would find it quite impossible to respond to these demands and would remain unconvinced that the successful product would be worth the potentially embarrassing process. For them, it must be said, the method would seem to be totally inappropriate. Its high cost and intensive method

Important considerations

of delivery would not, moreover, allow easy incorporation into the standard adult education programme. It is, nevertheless, a method that is finding increasing favour worldwide and deserves serious consideration.

Conclusion   We have examined in this unit a range of additional materials that can be used to aid the learning process, and a variety of techniques and approaches that can be employed to encourage learners to move from controlled to creative language use, and thus become better prepared for communication outside the classroom.

References

1. Hill, B, *Making the most of video*, CILT (1989).

2. Hill, N, 'Realia in the classroom', in Jones, B (ed), *Using authentic resources in teaching French,* CILT (1984).

3. Wright, A, Betteridge, D and M Buckby, *Games for language learning,* CUP (1984).

4-5. Greenall, S, *Language games and activities*, Hulton (1984).

6. Rinvolucri, M, *Grammar games*, CUP (1984).

7. Hadfield, J, *Harrap's communication games,* Nelson (1984).

8. Shiels, D, *France extra: guide for teachers*, BBC Publications (1985).

9-10. Littlewood, W, *Communicative language teaching*, CUP (1981).

11. Jones, K, *Designing your own simulations*, Methuen (1985).

12. Littlewood, see (9-10).

13. Kay, J, 'Songs and Singers', in Jones, B (ed), *Using authentic resources in teaching French,* CILT (1984).

14-15. Krashen, S D, *Principles and practice in second language acquisition,* Pergamon (1982).

16. Stevick, E, 'Suggestopedia: activating the student's reserve capacities', (1991). Revised and adapted from an article in *Forum,* 1985.

17. Gold, L, 'Suggestopedia: activating the students' reserve capacities', (1991). Revised and adapted from an article in *Forum,* 1985.

18-19. Fletcher, M, *A suggestopedic exploration of the elephant,* 1990.

20-23. Gold, see (17).

Further reading on communicative activities

Hamilton, J and J Clearie (French)/P Wheeldon (German), *Take your partners: pairwork exercises,* Macmillan (1985).

Klippel, F, *Keep talking,* CUP (1984).

Maley, A and A Duff, *Drama techniques in language learning,* CUP (1978).

Murray, T, *Role-play revision for GCSE French/Spanish*; Benbow, G, *Role-play revision for GCSE German,* Cassell (1990).

Pattison, P, *Developing communication skills,* CUP (1987).

Sidwell, D, *Toi et Moi (French), Du und Ich (German),* Nelson (1987/88).

Further reading on suggestopedia

Lozanov, G, *Suggestology and outlines of suggestopedy,* Gordon and Breach (1978).

Lozanov, G and E Gateva, *The foreign language teacher's suggestopedic manual,* Gordon and Breach (1988).

1.   Devise a role-play or simulation suitable for a class of fourteen learners at intermediate level. Be precise about aims and objectives.

2.   Choose a song recorded in the language you teach. Devise methods of exploiting it linguistically and/or thematically. How would you integrate it into your lesson plan?

Start compiling sets of songs, under structured headings noting down ways in which they could be used. Allow for cross-referencing linguistically and thematically.

3.   Adapt one of the following well-known TV or party games to suit a class that you teach:

Call my bluff
Blankety blank
Blockbusters
What's my line?
Charades

→ state your aims and the anticipated learning outcomes
→ outline how you would set up the game
→ what benefits/problems do you envisage?
→ how will you involve all the learners?

4.   Consider in what way(s) the suggestopedic method might be appropriate for a class you teach. What strategies do you adopt to ensure as far as possible a stress-free environment for your learners?

5.   Take one language function, e.g. finding your way around, and devise three integrated activities using different technologies to engage your learners and ensure adequate practice of the required language structures.

Extending the professional context 4

Course design for special purposes

Lore Arthur

This unit will look at the various aspects which a tutor should consider when designing a course, writing a syllabus and devising a scheme of work for a special purpose. This may be a course in a language for which little published material is available, a course which falls outside the conventional curriculum or, indeed, a tailor-made one designed for teaching in industry or commerce.

Most courses within adult/further or higher education follow a particular curriculum. In addition, in most instances the teaching is based on a particular coursebook which in practice lays down the course content. However, there are numerous languages for which no adequate published material is available. Juxtaposed, there are numerous students and organisations with specific needs, often work-related, which need individual attention and hence tailor-made course design.

Designing a course may be a complex enterprise but it is also a very practical one. In essence all course designs propose a programme of activities so that

The planning process

desired goals can be reached within the time available. The goals, then, are intended outcomes of the teaching-learning activities[1]. These are underpinned by a set of assumptions, values and beliefs which need to be clarified early on in the planning process so that misunderstandings can be avoided and the learning can be as effective and enjoyable as possible. Furthermore, the educational provider - that is, the head of department, the tutor organiser, or the company director who pays for the language training - will have another set of intentions and values related to that particular organisation of which the tutor needs to be aware.

It is generally the task of the tutor, however, to plan and organise a cohesive and balanced series of learning activities in such a way that all these goals can be achieved. A well planned course, therefore, with a good course design with clearly stated aims and objectives, appropriate resources and teaching materials provides the structural framework in which effective learning can take place.

If we consider the planning process as a whole we find it involves:

★ defining the target group (or individual), the learning needs, the overall aim and specific learning objectives;

★ devising a syllabus (course outline), a scheme of work (that is, a breakdown of topics laid down in the syllabus), lesson plans for each lesson (see unit 8);

★ Evaluating each lesson, the scheme of work, the whole course.

Planning a new course

Imagine you, as the tutor, have been asked to teach a particular course you have not taught before and you have to begin the planning process. Having sorted out the practical aspects, such as where and when the course will take place, and this may take serious consideration, the main questions must be:

★ for whom?
★ why and how?
★ with what?

The learner

For whom is the course? For a group or for an individual? Units 1-3 stress the diversity of adult learners; in any group there is likely to be a range of intellectual ability, language levels and linguistic aptitude. As previously stated, learners will come from different social and cultural backgrounds. In addition, the nature of the institution or organisation itself, its location, culture, purpose and environment will serve as an indicator for the likely student group.

Arabic for Business Purposes

GCSE Spanish

Getting by in Greek

Legal French in the Business Context

Turkish for Turkish-Speakers

Fashion Design in Italian

The why needs a little more reflection. It refers in this instance to the general aim of each language course. *Aims*

For example, the aim might be expressed in the following way:

Learning Spanish for Work-Related Purposes.

This course is aimed at absolute beginners wishing to communicate with a degree of ease and confidence with native speakers when working in Spain.

Why should learners wish to communicate with native speakers?

- so that they can obtain work;
- so that they speak, understand and read Spanish needed for work purposes;
- so that they get to know the Spanish way of life, country and culture and in due course they can make friends with speakers of Spanish.

A tall order indeed. It follows that the teacher will also have to be concerned about the how.

How can this be achieved? What should the course contain so that these aims can be fulfilled? What kind of language skills are needed? What kind of cultural background knowledge would ease the process of mutual understanding? And very specifically: What kind of topics, functions, structures and grammatical points should this course contain? Should all four skills be practised in equal proportions? What are the most appropriate methods? What are the most appropriate materials and resources? What do I, as a teacher, have to learn so that I can teach this course? *Content*

To make sense of all these different aspects one can devise a plan which covers:

☐ Intentions	aims (general), goals (specific)
☐ Language content	themes, topics, settings, functions, language structures, vocabulary, grammar
☐ Language skills	listening, speaking, reading, writing, integration of skills - and prioritising
☐ Timing	beginning, middle and end of course, route of progression, achievement of objectives according to scheme of work
☐ Methods	precommunicative/communicative/tutor-led - or student-led/discussions/questioning/group or pair work, role-play, games, drilling/snowballing/ dictation /gap-filling amongst others

☐ Materials	Videos, cassettes, overhead projectors, flipcharts, maps, cue cards, authentic materials, coursebooks, cultural background/information materials amongst others
☐ Other resources	experience/knowledge the teacher has, the learners bring into the classroom, the organisation provides, colleagues and other professional bodies can offer
☐ Testing	revision, informal and formal testing, student progress reports, achievement charts, end of course examinations
☐ Reassessment	monitoring, adjusting schemes of work at regular intervals throughout the course
☐ Evaluation	student evaluation of whole course, teacher evaluation of lessons, and of course, both formal and informal

Syllabus

All this may be written up into a course outline or syllabus, which can be handed to the institution or company, and in some instances to the prospective student. It should, therefore, contain all the relevant information a student or a colleague may need and should be written in a clear, jargon-free manner covering most of the aspects outlined above.

Scheme of work

A scheme of work, on the other hand, means in practice providing more detailed information on one or several form sheets which is broken down into specific sections. Many institutions provide their own forms and have their own house style. Others expect tutors to submit a syllabus and design their own scheme of work as part of their employment contract (see p 118 for example). All this may sound very daunting at first. However, almost all colleagues and employers are willing to help. It needs to be stressed at this point that all plans, including a scheme of work or a single lesson plan, need to be monitored, reassessed and adjusted throughout the course according to the needs and wishes of the learners.

Foreign Language Training in Industry (FLTI)

Most adult education centres or further/higher education colleges now offer language courses to individuals or groups who need a foreign language for a particular work-related purpose in the context of industry and commerce. They may also be attached to a local LX-Centre (Languages and Export Centres are consortia initially set up by the Government in response to increasing foreign language needs within the context of a Single European Market). The aim is to stimulate and respond to a wide range of language learning needs which cannot be accommodated in a more conventional setting.

Case study

Ms X is a company marketing manager for a British company selling table linen in Italy. She needs to travel from time to time to Italy to discuss promotion campaigns, advertising and selling arrangements amongst other things with Italian clients. In the course of time she has picked up some Italian, that is, she understands a little and can speak a few words, enough to get by when travelling. She has at times tried to teach herself but with little success. She has never been taught Italian formally, but she studied

French up to 'A' Level standard many years ago. Ms X has very little time available. Her company will pay for a tailor-made course with individual tuition.

Clearly, Ms X has very specific needs which do not easily fit into a more conventional curriculum. She needs above all 'social language', that is, not the language of a tourist abroad but that required for socialising in a business context, as do the majority of FLTI learners[2]. Furthermore, she is likely to need oral/aural skills rather than reading and writing ones. She should be able to progress rapidly, having learnt French to a good standard at school. She is likely to be determined and should probably cope well with independent study in addition to the tuition, provided she received guidance. Because of her hectic working day she is unlikely to be able to join any classes and will, therefore, need teaching on a one-to-one basis. All this cannot be established without a proper needs analysis.

Needs analysis

The needs of the learner(s), as we have seen above, dictate the teaching objectives and the course design. It follows, therefore, that the learning needs of the individual learner or group of learners have to be clearly identified in a formal way before the planning process can begin. For example, a business manager who regularly deals with foreign clients will require different language skills to those of a secretary whose main task is to deal with telephone enquiries at home[3].

Special concerns

There are other aspects which are of concern to many language teachers new to teaching in industry and commerce, such as:

- *teaching technical language*: this is not nearly such a problem as assumed - teachers are not expected to be experts in any professional field other than their own; companies are usually willing to help; most learners can cope with technical words in the target language before they can speak 'social language', for example.

- *appropriate teaching materials*: much authentic material (brochures, charts, leaflets) can be obtained from within the company and can be adjusted for teaching purposes according to the needs of the learner(s); in addition, there is an increasing number of commercially available textbooks in a variety of languages suitable for FLTI.

- *teaching one to one*: this necessitates different pace and intensity from group tuition, particular attention to individual learning style and allows materials to be used not suitable for group tuition.

- *fees*: many tutors do not know how much to charge for private tuition either in their own homes or on the premises in the company. Language tutors offer a professional service and should be rewarded appropriately. Hourly tuition rates offered by adult education centres may serve as a guideline. Included in the fee should be extra time spent on preparation, travelling, possible income tax and additional expenses incurred. A cancellation fee should also be negotiated.

As we have seen, the world of language teaching is becoming increasingly rich in its diversity. Professional language teachers are no longer just teaching languages, they also manage and organise, counsel and guide,

The expanding context

assess and evaluate, and respond and adjust to a complex and changing set of demands (see unit 17).

In a multicultural, multilingual society such as ours, and against the background of the European Community, it is no longer appropriate to say that *it is possible to be a civilised and educated person while speaking and understanding English... Only a few of us need to be competent in foreign languages - for diplomacy, marketing and other special purposes*[4]. Instead, the words of John McGregor, former Secretary of State for Education, are more relevant nowadays:

> *Competence in modern foreign languages is an imperative. It is critical to our ability to establish and maintain trading and cultural links with other countries. We simply must extend the ability of our young people to speak foreign languages.*[5]

References

1. Rogers, A, *Teaching adults*, Open University (1986).

2. Scullard, S, *The provision of foreign language training to industry for the FHE provider*, Further Education Unit (1989).

3. LCCI, *The non-specialist use of foreign languages in industry and commerce*, LCCI Examinations Board (1985).

4. Rigby, G and R Burgess, *Language teaching in Higher Education*, Department Employment Group (1992).

5. Rigby and Burgess, see (4).

Recommended reading

Embleton, D and S Hagen, *Languages in international business: a practical guide*, Hodder and Stoughton (1992).

Haeften, K van, *Language training for industry and the role of open learning*, National Council for Educational Technology (1991).

Jones, R, *Languages and how to master them*, Allborough Publishing (1991).

Murphey, T, *Teaching one to one*, Longman (1991).

Wilberg, P, *One to one*, Language Teaching Publications (1987).

Please note: many language teaching bookshops stock suitable books under the section *English for special purposes*. The foreign language teacher may wish to adapt these for his/her own needs.

Over to you

Task: Discuss the points below; see if you can add some.

TEACHING ONE TO ONE

1. Go at student's own pace

2. Be in genuine communication with student all the time (don't set meaningless tasks for your own sake)

3. Adjust to different personalities and learning styles

4. Monitor student's communication, progress and errors on a continuous basis

5. Allow student to take charge of own learning as much as possible (own in tray, for example, control of cassette recorder, choice of materials)

6. Gather and prepare material to suit student, including self-access material

7. Plan with students and allow choices

8. Use biographical and work-related information for intensive language work

9. Make extensive use of close-up aids such as cards, cuisaire rods

10. Encourage student to collect authentic materials, charts, diagrams, etc from his/her company which can then be used for teaching

11. Encourage student to monitor/evaluate his/her own progress at all times

Thanks to Elizabeth Clifton, Pedagogical Director, Linguarama.

SCHEME OF WORK for a tailor-made course
(an example)

Class title: _____ Time/Day: _____

Aims of course: _____

_____

Learning outcomes: _____

_____

Content	Week 1	Week 2
Topics/themes		
Functions		
Structures		
Grammar		

Task: Evaluate this checklist; imagine you have been asked to prepare a course for a commercial company. This course will be very expensive and your planning needs to be very thorough. How could you extend and improve this list and hence your own preparation?

CHECKLIST

Course title:

Do I have/know... Are/is there ...	No	More	Enough	Task accomplished
... information about company/ students				
... all the details re time and location				
... information about rooms/resources available in-house, i.e. OHP, board, video, etc				
... about the topics to be taught				
... materials for course itself?				

Unit 15

Developing independent learning

Doreen Markham

This unit seeks to define concepts of independent learning and its development in conjunction with modern teaching resources. It examines how such resources, including self-access systems, work and how the teacher can guide and help the learner.

What do we mean by independent learning?

The past two decades have seen radical changes in modes of learning, with the switch to active, learner-centred, resource-based classroom techniques. Simultaneously, ever more sophisticated electronic media have been developed and are making an increasingly valuable contribution to the learning process. Research into distance learning has revealed the benefits of a diversified input, whilst pedagogical research would indicate that learning is ineffectual if the learner is totally dependent on the teacher and taking no responsibility for his or her own learning.

The logical outcome of this has been the growing importance of supported self-study, which can be defined as independent study, based on the use of resources, and accompanying conventional face-to-face tuition. The learner is moving towards greater autonomy, becoming increasingly responsible for taking initiatives and decisions, whilst the teacher is required more and more to assume the role of guide and counsellor. This should be distinguished from self-tuition, or self-instruction, which excludes the teacher and consequently the opportunity for interaction. Communication is so inherent a part of language learning that any apprenticeship which depends solely on resources, however 'interactive' they may be, cannot be entirely satisfactory. Supported self-study, then, is situated mid-way on a spectrum extending from self-tuition to intensive one-to-one tutoring. Definitions and terminology vary, but all share the common concept of the learner actively planning and deciding, no longer passively obeying the teacher's instructions[1].

Resources

Audio cassettes

Audio cassettes, offering the advantages of flexibility, diversity and cheapness, are by far the most popular resource for the adult learner, who is easily convinced of their usefulness in enhancing his/her chances of successful communication in the foreign language. Cassettes for listening purposes are simple to use and can be loaned or purchased, for use at home, in the car or on a personal stereo. Alternatively, they can be used interactively in the language laboratory, or on audio-active comparative 'mini-labs'. As with the booths in the language laboratory, these function on two parallel tracks, enabling the student to listen to a master track whilst recording on the student track. Thus, the student is prompted to speak and practise the sounds and, although self-criticism has been shown to be of limited efficiency, and a perfect recording does not imply competent interaction, any speech is better than no speech. Mini-labs - together with a fast copier if funds will allow - are a relatively cheap method of equipping a resources centre (far cheaper than a language laboratory) and have the added appeal for adults of greater privacy[2].

There is a vast range of material available in the major languages: recordings to accompany tutored methods which can be used outside class time for reinforcement and revision; courses designed for self-tuition but which constitute a useful adjunct to any course. Edited authentic materials, such as *Authentik* and BBC broadcasts for schools, or indeed, off-air recordings, simple enough to obtain with a radio-cassette player from nearby European countries or during visits to the country, are suitable for individual study if accompanied by transcript and worksheets. The self-tuition courses range from the more traditional methods providing oral drilling in the structures of the language[3] to the modern multi-media packages based on authentic dialogues and a functional/notional approach. The BBC is currently extending their range of languages, and their materials are easy to obtain[4].

Video

Video is increasingly becoming standard equipment in language teaching, popularised by the highly successful BBC TV series: *A vous la France*, *Deutsch Direkt* and *España viva*, amongst others. Many of these are now commercially available on VHS, as are an increasing number of multi-media courses incorporating books, audio and video cassettes. Worth noting are those being produced by language centres and 'LX' (Language and Export - see unit 14) centres, aimed at the business market and concentrating on skills such as telephoning and negotiating. The market is, however, expanding. It is worth exploring new material all the time. Video does not (as yet) allow for verbal responses on the part of the learner, but is a very effective medium of language instruction in combining sound, graphics and the written word with a wealth of visual information about the speaker, the context, non-verbal elements of communication and the socio-cultural background. The ideal viewing equipment is the small video presenter, which can be used with or without individual headphones and which has a playback facility allowing the student to work through the programme and accompanying exercises at his/her own pace.

Satellite television is now becoming more accessible and we are moving into a period when many, or even the majority of language centres have satellite TV at their disposal. A range of packages exists, according to the number of programmes and languages required, via a satellite dish or cable according to area. For most purposes, 'Eutelsat' will provide ample material with channels in the major European languages (three German, two Italian, one Spanish and one French, i.e. TV5 which combines programmes from several French-speaking countries), while the monthly *Satellite TV Europe*, available through newsagents, provides programme schedules[5]. The main problem will undoubtedly prove to be the handling and organising of the abundance of material on offer, as sorting, editing and preparing are all very time-consuming. Direct access to satellite TV is not advisable for security reasons, so a VCR (Video Cassette Recorder), with timer, is essential equipment for recording broadcasts which will subsequently be used by students. Initially, one can start by regularly recording news and current affairs in each language and quite simply making these available to students. News items are relatively brief and accessible to the student dealing with current affairs. One can gradually build up a library of less ephemeral materials with accompanying work (and answer) sheets for future reference. Such recordings lend themselves to a variety of activities, ranging from the simple grid (who? where? what? why? when?) to more complex substitution, transcription and reformulation exercises[6].

Computer software has taken somewhat longer to introduce, encountering resistance because of its complexity from both adult learners and part-time tutors, on whom so many language centres depend. However, as more adults become familiar with Information Technology, and more teachers are trained in CALL, computers will certainly play a greater part in language training.

Computer-Assisted Language Learning (CALL)

Software currently available can be divided into several categories. Firstly, programs providing language exercises, such as practice in points of grammar (transformation and substitution exercises) or in vocabulary (cloze tests). Many of these come in the form of authoring programs, where the teacher inputs the texts or exercises required. Some courses now include computer software in a multi-media package (*Spain after Franco, A vous la France*, etc) or even offer a complete course of tuition on computer (e.g. TopWare's *Euro* series). The other main use of the computer is as a source of authentic material from a database, which many adults will be required to handle in their work.

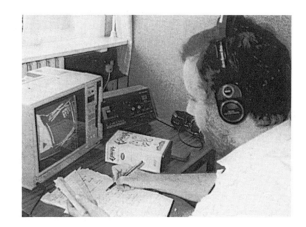

Many colleges subscribe to databases such as *Campus 2000*, or even the French *Télétel* service, but for the teacher who has no access to such facilities, software is published containing viewdata material. The National Council for Educational Technology (NCET) provides full information on services and software[7].

The advantage of the computer is that learners can, without embarrassment, work as slowly or as quickly as they wish, have the constant individual attention of the 'tutor' and the possibility of instantaneous correction. A rapid interaction is set up, the learner responding to a stimulus on the screen via the keyboard, and the computer reacting to this by presenting another stimulus. Emphasis is placed on the learner monitoring him/herself and calling up help or guidance, but the computer may also be programmed to 'branch' the learner to correct answers and explanations[7]. The drawback is, of course, that all this is based on the written language alone, but recent developments are attempting to solve this problem. Interactive video combines the advantages of video and the computer, providing TV quality vision and sound whilst allowing for (non-oral) interaction from the student. Software is currently being developed which integrates sound and will eventually allow the learner to record his/her oral responses and compare them to a master recording as in the language laboratory[8].

Management of resources

The resources centre may be within a larger language centre in a university or polytechnic, part of a languages section in a college of further education or an adult education centre, in a private language school, or in a company. Many businesses are now setting up language centres as part of their language training schemes, having realised that staff will benefit more from tuition if they have ready access to study facilities; in many instances they turn to their local training provider for advice. Similarly, colleges involved in business training will find that a 'package' which includes time spent on resources will be more attractive to a firm's training officer who will see this as better 'value for money'.

The term 'self-access centre' covers a variety of situations and systems. At one extreme, we find the library style resource centre, in its own premises and with the latest equipment, well stocked with materials and staffed by technicians, secretaries, librarians and teacher/helpers. This, of course, requires capital investment and most smaller institutions, faced with problems of staffing and funding, make do with less.

Other, more modest solutions are possible, and a step-by-step approach is likely to appear less daunting. It is worth bearing in mind that, in the first instance, a resources centre need not involve open access to materials, need not be open on a permanent basis and need not have specialist staffing. The following suggestions[9] may serve as a starting point:

- a loan system, with materials stored in a secure place with staff-only access and loaned out for use elsewhere on the premises or at home;
- a teaching room such as a language laboratory, used as a classroom most of the time and as a self-access centre, under staff supervision, at certain times (lunch, or twilight);
- an open-access room not under direct supervision, with basic equipment, materials such as periodicals and a catalogue of more valuable materials available elsewhere from a member of staff.

Whatever the solution, creating a centre needs thorough planning, and it is important to allow time not only for the initial equipping and stocking of the centre, but also for maintaining, cataloguing, producing and updating materials, as well as for training part-timers to make full use of the centre.

Materials should be built up gradually, starting with newspapers, magazines, other printed realia and worksheets originally designed for class use, before moving on to audio cassettes, videos and computer programs - and accompanying hardware. A clear cataloguing system is essential, and care should be taken to provide a balanced range of materials catering for different levels, skills and interests. In this respect, a subscription to *Authentik*[10] is a simple way of constituting a stock of newspaper articles, radio recordings (with transcriptions) and worksheets, well suited for independent study and covering a wide variety of topics at various levels.

The teacher's role

Contrary to some initial misconceptions, self-access systems do not dispense with the need for qualified teachers. The teacher's role, however, is changing from that of 'instructor' to that of 'guide', 'counsellor' and 'facilitator', whose task is to train the learner and help develop his/her capacity for independent learning[11]. This role will differ according to whether the teacher is 'resource-based', i.e. a counsellor attached primarily to the self-access centre[12], or is a tutor who is guiding the learner towards appropriate learning strategies outside class contact time. As we see, *most schemes designed to promote autonomous language learning among adults are founded on a combination of learning resources and learner counselling*[13] and in both cases the teacher's aim is to train the learner to learn more effectively.

As **counsellor**, the teacher will help the learner to[14]:

- analyse his/her needs in the foreign language;
- understand his/her personal learning strategies;
- establish targets and a programme of work;
- devise a system of checks to measure success.

This can be achieved by discussion, but assessment sheets, completed prior to a personal interview, can be more efficient since, by asking the learner to reflect on a certain number of questions, they are already encouraging him/her to take the first step on the road to autonomy.

As **guide**, the teacher will need to ascertain that the learner has mastered the basic skills required to use resources, catalogues, indexes, etc and can find material in the centre. Secondly, the teacher will need to give advice and answer queries on level and needs assessment, on study plans and monitoring of results. To achieve this, familiarity with the resources is essential, and ideally, all teachers will be encouraged to contribute materials for use in the centre[15].

As with all innovations, the introduction of self-access facilities takes time and energy, and brings its rewards, not least of which are well-organised resources also available for classwork, and a more inviting and varied 'homework' programme ready for use.

References

1. For further discussion of these terms, see Dickinson, L, *Self-instruction in language learning*, CUP (1987) and Little, D, *Learner autonomy*, Authentik (1991).

2. Barley, A, *Making the most of audio*, CILT (1990).

3. Linguaphone, for example, which covers many of the otherwise unavailable minority languages.

4. For example, the *Get by series: Get by in Arabic/Chinese/Greek/Japanese/Portuguese/Turkish* etc.

5. Coleman, J, 'Starting with satellite: a basic guide to using off-air video recordings in the language classroom', *ALL Language Learning Journal*, (September 1990), pp16-18.

6. For fuller details, see Hill, B, *Making the most of satellites and interactive video*, CILT (1991).

7. National Council for Educational Technology, Science Park, Coventry CV4 7EZ. Issues *Information Sheets* (free) on the use of computers in the teaching of modern languages.

8. Davies, G and J J Higgins (eds), *Computers, language and language learning*, CILT (1983).

9. Little, D, *Self-access systems for language learning*, Authentik/CILT (1989) and Dickinson, see (1).

10. *Authentik* newspapers and cassettes in French, German, Spanish and English published five times a year. Full details from: Authentik, 27 Westland Square, Dublin 2.

11. Sheerin, S, *Self-access*, OUP (1989), chapter 2.

12. See details of organisation of the Cambridge Open Access Sound and Video Library in Dickinson, see (1).

13. Little, D in Gathercole, I (ed), *Autonomy in language learning*, CILT (1990), p 11.

14. Little, D, *Learner autonomy*, Authentik (1991), p 7.

15. Sheerin, see (11).

Further reading

Barley, A, *Making the most of audio,* CILT (1990).

Davies, G, and J J Higgins (eds), *Computers, language and language learning,* CILT (1983).

Dickinson, L, *Self-instruction in language learning,* CUP (1987).

Ellis, G and B Sinclair, *Learning to learn English,* CUP (1989).

Gathercole, I (ed), *Autonomy in language learning,* CILT (1990).

Hewer, S, *Making the most of IT skills,* CILT (1989).

Hill, B, *Making the most of video,* CILT (1989).

Hill, B, *Making the most of satellites and interactive video,* CILT (1991).

Little, D, *Self-access systems for language learning,* Authentik/CILT (1989).

Little, D, *Learner autonomy,* Authentik (1991).

Lonergan, J, *Making the most of your video camera,* CILT (1990).

Page, B (ed), *Letting go, taking hold - a guide to independent language learning by teachers for teachers,* CILT (1992).

Rendall, H, *Making the most of micro-computers,* CILT (1991).

Sheerin, S, *Self-access,* OUP (1989).

Over to you

Situations for discussion:

1. A local firm for whom you have been providing language training, has just been taken over by a German company and has come to you for advice on setting up a resources centre. Money is generous but not limitless (approximately £2,500). What equipment and materials would you suggest?

2. You have recently set up a self-access centre and have obtained funding for a half-day training session with part-time tutors so that they will make better use of the resources and contribute to the creation and renewal of materials. Plan a programme for the event.

   Setting up a self-access centre in your institution: how would you deal with the following issues?

   → rooming, staffing, equipment, security, opening hours.

   Study the introduction of one resource to your centre, such as satellite television news, from the following points of view: obtaining material, editing, informing and advising students on use, preparing support documents.

Unit 16

Testing language performance

Susan Ainslie

This unit discusses the purposes of testing, defines different types of test, suggests criteria to be applied when designing and administering classroom tests, and considers the tests available through external bodies.

Testing is one way of assessing our students' progress and the effectiveness of our teaching. We can also assess our students' progress by spot questions and homework. Testing can include:

What do we mean by testing?

★ a ten-minute informal quiz to check that the learning objectives of, for example, last week's lesson have been achieved;

★ a global test at, say, termly intervals to check on overall progress made;

★ a formal examination accredited externally by regional, national or international bodies such as an Open Learning Federation, a Graded Testing Unit, the Royal Society of Arts, or the International Certificate Conference. (see below)

Most of us are involved at some stage in the design and administration of tests and in the selection of suitable forms of accreditation for our students. The reasons for testing vary, and it is important for us to be clear as to why we want to administer a test at any particular point in a course, and to be sure that the test we administer does test what we want it to test. In order to be able to do this we need to understand some of the basic principles behind testing.

The initial reaction of adult education tutors and students alike to the suggestion that they are working towards some form of accreditation can be hostile, to say the least. *Adults don't like being tested; adult education is about leisure and pleasure, so why put the students through the ordeal of being tested?; the vast majority of adult students have no need or use for any sort of qualification.* The terror on the face of the enrolling beginner on being told that the course leads to some sort of a test confirms the teacher in this view. And at enrolment, if you would like the student to come to the first lesson, let alone the rest of the course, it would be a good idea to say that the test is entirely optional!

Why test?

There are a number of **good reasons for testing**, however, and research suggests that 80% of adult students do not object to being tested anyway[1]. The reasons for testing given below are not necessarily in order of importance.

- **Diagnostic**. It is important for us to know that our learners are achieving the aims and objectives of our course. We need to be able to identify their strengths and weaknesses, in order to be able to plan the rest of the course to meet their needs. We need to check that our teaching has been successful. It is also helpful for the student to know what he/she has and has not mastered.

- **Motivation**. It is well known that the most important single factor in foreign language learning success is motivation. One sort of motivation comes from the sense of achievement from having succeeded in a test, and is one of the reasons behind the success of the Graded Testing movement. Having reached one goal, students are encouraged to continue towards the next one.

- Formal testing, or accreditation as it is often called, helps to provide a **coherent framework and structure** so that learners who wish to do so can progress from a beginners' level up to an advanced level over a number of years. Adult education organisations are often spread over a number of centres, with several people involved in making decisions about what to offer students. If teachers agree on a line of progression, students are less likely to complain, for example, that at the end of year 2 there was such a big jump to what the teacher was doing in year 3 that they could not keep up and dropped out. HMI reported that

  > external examinations ensure unity of purpose and greater consistency of achievement.[2]

- **Qualifications** are becoming increasingly important, and evidence of having attained a certain level of proficiency will enhance prospects of employment for our students. We would be doing them a disservice if we did not offer them the opportunity to become formally qualified if that is what they wish. Formal recognition of achievement will be particularly important for the increasing number of our students who may be expected to work abroad in years to come.

Reasons for not testing

While there are a number of good reasons for testing, it can also have a negative effect. Too much insistence on testing can put undue pressure on our students, spoil their enjoyment and be demotivating. And while success in tests is motivating, how many of our students are **not** going to succeed, and what will be the effect on them? This is one reason for the popularity of tests which mark positively, awarding marks for achievement rather than deducting marks for failure. And it is also why it is the intention of designers of tests like City and Guilds and the Graded Tests that students should not enter for them until they are ready to pass them.

It is very important to choose tests which will assess what we feel to be appropriate learning goals for our students. The backwash effect of tests is well known and can be harmful or beneficial.

If a test is regarded as important, then preparation for it can come to dominate all teaching and learning activities. And if the test content and testing techniques are at variance with the objectives of the course, then there is likely to be harmful backwash.[3]

If, for example, we choose as our test one that places great emphasis on written accuracy and only allocates a small percentage of the marks to oral performance, we as teachers will tend to place the same sort of emphasis on classroom activities. Hughes discusses ways of achieving beneficial backwash, including testing the abilities which you want to develop and encourage, sampling widely and unpredictably, testing directly the skills you wish to foster, making tests criterion-referenced, basing achievement tests on objectives rather than content, and ensuring the demands of the test are known and understood by students and teachers[4].

Tests should aim to be both **valid** and **reliable**. A valid test is one which measures accurately what it is supposed to measure. There are different sorts of validity. A test which has **content validity** contains a representative sample of the language skills, structures, etc which it is meant to test. **Criterion-related validity** means that results gained in a test agree with another independent form of assessment of the candidate. **Construct validity** measures the ability it is supposed to measure and nothing else[5]. Heaton cites an example of a test which lacks construct validity:

Basic principles of language testing: validity and reliability

A composition test which requires students to write about modern methods of transport may not be valid since it will measure not only an ability to write in English but also an interest in, or a knowledge of, modern transport.[6]

A reliable test is one which would produce virtually the same results if administered on two separate occasions. As Hughes says:

*What we have to do is construct, administer and score tests in such a way that the scores actually obtained on a particular occasion are likely to be **very similar** to those which would have been obtained if it had been administered to the same students with the same ability, but at a different time.*[7]

Valette specifies four factors that contribute to a test's reliability:

Standard tasks *(all candidates answer the same questions);* **standard conditions** *(all candidates take the test in the same context and are given the same amount of time to respond to the questions);* **multiple tasks** *(there are many questions, so as to provide a broad sampling of the candidates' knowledge);* **standard scoring** *(all tests are scored the same way, so that the score would not change if the paper were marked by a second evaluator).*[8]

Objectivity is clearly a key feature of a reliable test, and multiple choice, true/false, and open-ended sentence completion questions have a high level of objectivity and are therefore examples of reliable tests. A reliable test, however, may not be valid, and there is a danger that in increasing reliability a test loses its validity. A multiple choice test, for example, is not a valid way of testing communicative competence. In practice, most tests are neither wholly valid nor wholly reliable, but strive to be as close as possible to both.

Different kinds of tests

The type of test we choose to administer will depend upon the information we want to obtain from it. We touched briefly above on **objective tests**. Tests can be objective or subjective according to the way in which they are marked. A test which requires the tester to make a judgement is subjective. It is difficult to test oral competence without some measure of subjective evaluation. In order to minimise the subjective element, numerical scores are often allocated to a number of criteria identified for evaluation, such as fluency, accent, comprehension and so on[9].

Tests can be **criterion-referenced** or **norm-referenced**. A norm-referenced test measures one student's performance against another's or against the rest of the group. If you happened to take your test in a year when everyone was above average you would lose out in this sort of test! Increasingly, however, tests are criterion-referenced. A criterion-referenced test measures performance against a list of defined criteria and it is possible to have a pass rate of 100% on this type of test. Graded Tests are an example of criterion-referenced tests.

A **proficiency test** measures what the student can do, irrespective of any syllabus or course; an **achievement test** measures what the student can do on the basis of a syllabus, and these tests may test progress or final achievement. Teachers are likely to set achievement tests rather than proficiency tests. **Discrete-point** testing specifies particular elements which are to be tested; an **integrative test** measures global achievement.

Testing communicative competence

Most language courses nowadays aim to develop communicative competence[10]. Tests of communicative competence aim to reproduce as closely as possible authentic situations which can be evaluated, and which take into account psycholinguistic and sociolinguistic features of language performance. Testees are required to perform operations at appropriate levels, choosing language that is suitable for the situation specified. Role-play almost invariably forms part of a test of communicative competence. Scorers need to be clear to what extent they insist on linguistic accuracy if effective communication has taken place.

Such tests pose two problems, however. First, any situation that is created for testing purposes cannot by definition be an authentic communicative situation. Secondly, there will inevitably be a gap between linguistic **competence** (what the student knows) and linguistic **performance** (what the student is able to produce), both because of the stressful nature of an oral test, and also because the test can only sample performance. To do otherwise would be very time-consuming and logistically impracticable.

Techniques for testing

As can be seen, test design and construction are not straightforward and can be very time-consuming. There is no space in this unit to discuss techniques for testing in detail; a few key points are mentioned, but reference is made at the end to some excellent sources of more detailed information. Many tests will include a number of the techniques specified below, and tests should always include several different tasks and test types in order to give a representative sample of the tasks we would expect the students to be able to perform. The way in which the tests are scored will reflect the purpose of a particular test item: do we want to analyse specific linguistic points, or are we more interested in the ability to communicate?

Multiple choice testing is used to test many language abilities, and has the advantage that scoring can be reliable and quick, and the testee can be expected to answer many items in a short time. The technique only tests recognition knowledge, however, and it is very difficult to write successful test items. This is because the **distracters** (i.e. the 'wrong' answers) should all be **plausible** alternatives to the correct answer, but there are not always three or four suitable alternatives. Multiple choice tests should always have four possible answers, as the possibility of guessing the right answer is too high if there are only three alternatives[11].

Task-based tests consider how well students can perform certain tasks using the foreign language. For example, can they understand and act on information given over the telephone? Can they extract information from a railway timetable in order to plan a journey? These tests focus on the ability to carry out successfully certain tasks rather than on linguistic accuracy per se, and they enable us to predict how well the students could perform the same or similar tasks in real life[12].

On the whole, if we wish to test a particular linguistic skill we ask our students to perform that skill. There are, however, some tests which can give a global overview of the student's general ability. **Dictation, cloze tests** and **C-tests** measure overall ability in a language. Research has revealed high correlations between scores on **dictation** tests and scores on much longer and more complex tests. **Cloze** tests leave blanks in a passage, requiring the testee to fill them in: usually this is every 9th, 11th, 15th word, depending on the level of our students. The random nature of these tests sometimes means that some of the answers are virtually impossible to guess, even by a native speaker. **C-tests** delete the second half of every second word, which reduces the likelihood of an answer being impossible to find. In all these tests, choice of appropriate texts is important. They are, however, easy to prepare, mark and administer, and give a reasonable estimate of overall ability[13].

Accreditation by external bodies

There are a number of different examining bodies at regional, national and international level which offer different forms of accreditation. The teacher faced with the decision as to which one to choose has a daunting task, and a useful meeting for teachers would be to obtain information from all the examining boards and evaluate the material against agreed criteria. (See the suggested activity at the end of this unit, though it is important to look critically at what the examination boards say.) As far as equivalent levels are concerned, however, fortunately the National Council for Vocational Qualifications has been producing definitions of modern foreign language competence at a number of levels, and comparative tables of NVQs and existing scales (see unit 12).

At the same time, under the auspices of the LINGUA programme, Action III, a European-wide initiative, is collecting information about available forms of accreditation throughout Europe[14].

LANGUAGE EXAMINATIONS: APPROXIMATE LEVELS

No. of hours in class	Proposed core skills/NVQ levels	Examinations	No. of hours in class
30		Graded tests Level 1	30
60		Graded tests Level 2 (just!); FLIC Preliminary	60
90			90
120	1 (Survival)	Graded tests Level 3; RSA Level 1; IOL Preliminary (Centra 2)	120
150		GCSE Basic	150
180	2 (Threshold)	GCSE Higher; RSA Level 2; IOL General	180
210		FLIC Threshold	210
240		AEB French for Business; RSA Level 3	240
270			270
300	3 (Lower)	'A' Level; FLIC Intermediate	300
		IOL Advanced (modular)	
	4 (Intermediate)	IOL Intermediate Diploma	
	5 (Higher)	Degree; IOL Diploma; FLIC Advanced	

+   Modern Language Skills for Work (St. Martin's) Basic + optional modules - profile statement
FLAW (Foreign Language Skills at Work) - LCCI assessed on a profile wheel - £80.00 to register
BTEC
City and Guilds Modern Language Schemes (First certification 1991)

IOL = Institute of Linguists   RSA = Royal Society of Arts

References

1. Arthur, L, *Study into independent language learning,* Goldsmiths' College (1990).

2. DES, *A survey of foreign language courses for adult students in 34 institutions,* a report by HMI, DES (1988).

3. Hughes, A, *Testing for language teachers,* CUP (1989), p 1.

4. Hughes, see (3), p 44.

5. Hughes, see (3), p 22.

6. Heaton, J B, *Classroom testing,* Longman (1990), p 7.

7. Hughes, see (3), p 29.

8. Valette, R M, 'Objective evaluation and transparency', in Freudenstein, R (ed), *Language learning,* AIMAV/Didier (1978), p 107.

9. Hughes, see (3), p 111-113.

10. See CILT information sheet *What is meant by a 'communicative approach to modern language teaching?',* CILT (1989).

11. Hughes, see (3), p 59.

12. Heaton, see (6), p 28.

13. Hughes, see (3), p 62-73.

14. For further information write to Tony Fitzpatrick, Deutscher Volkshochschulverband, 6000 Frankfurt 1, Holzhausenstr 21.

Over to you

1. *A framework for courses*

Consider the following framework of courses which is in place at a college in Lancashire.
NB A year consists usually of 30 two-hour lessons.

End of year 1:   Graded tests levels 1 or 2 depending on students (often 1 plus part of 2).

End of year 2:   Graded tests level 3 (Lancs and Cumbria).

End of year 3:   RSA 1 or GCSE (group/tutor decides).

End of year 4:   RSA 2 or moving towards 'AS'/'A' level.

End of year 5:   RSA 3.

After this level there is an advanced diploma available at the local polytechnic, up to approximately degree level.

Compare this with your own structure if you have one, or discuss whether or not you feel it would be appropriate for you.

2. *Selecting appropriate forms of accreditation*

You will need to get hold of syllabuses from the different examining boards for this exercise.

a. Look at the following list of criteria for the selection of appropriate forms of accreditation (adapted from a list used by teachers in Lancashire and Cheshire).

★ does it test communicative competence?
★ is it adult-orientated?
★ does it avoid racist and sexist language?
★ are the aims/objectives/skills appropriate?
★ is the content general or business-related?

To make it attractive to the learners

★ is it reasonably priced?
★ is it flexible? can it be taken at any time?
★ is it nationally/internationally recognised? Does it fit in with NVQs?

To make it attractive to teachers/organisers

★ are suitable teaching materials readily available?
★ is it easy/straightforward to administer?
★ is the examination board efficient?
★ is it available in all languages?

b. Do you agree with this list for your situation? If not, modify it accordingly.

c. Having agreed your set of criteria, look at the different examination boards' materials and assess to what extent they meet the criteria.

d. Choose the forms of assessment most appropriate for your students.

3. *Examinations*

Get hold of some past papers or specimen papers from the examining boards.

Select at random some of the questions and ask yourself the following questions.

★ What is the purpose of the test?
★ How is it achieved?
★ Is the task realistic?
★ What would be the backwash effect of this type of test?
★ Do you think that this test is an appropriate one?
★ How long would it take to administer this test?

Unit 17

Being a professional

Susan Ainslie

This unit discusses what 'being a professional' implies, and suggests ways of raising standards of professionalism. It points out the need for continual updating and self-evaluation. It examines the responsibilities of managers and organisers as well as the teachers themselves in providing a professional service for our students.

What does 'being a professional' mean?

'Being a professional' encompasses all aspects of teaching foreign languages to adults. It means possessing knowledge and being able to transmit it to others, being able to create an environment in which learning takes place. It means keeping up to date linguistically, theoretically, and with developments in technology. It means providing a **quality** service to our students; 'doing a good job'. The other side of the coin is that there should be a structure to enable teachers to obtain appropriate qualifications.

Knowledge of the subject

The implications for the adult education tutor are considerable and of continuing importance. First, **knowledge** of a language means more than just knowing the lexis and structures; a language is part of a culture, and language and culture are constantly changing and developing. Native speakers who live abroad can lose their up-to-date knowledge of the language and also of the changing contexts within which that language is used. Non-native speakers with degrees in languages may have a fossilised knowledge of the language they studied a number of years ago. The situations in which it is appropriate to use familiar forms of address, for example, have changed considerably since I was a language student. As teachers we owe it to our learners to maintain close contact with the living language and with the way of life and cultural and social changes in the country whose language we teach.

The theoretical background

In addition to knowledge of our subject, we need to know how to transmit it to others. In order to succeed in this task, teachers need to have an understanding of:

★ how learning takes place;
★ how language learning takes place;
★ how adults learn.

If we do not have these insights, we have no basis upon which to make decisions about what we do in our classrooms. We are sailing a boat without a rudder[1]. And as theories and knowledge are constantly developing and being modified, we need, again, to keep abreast of change.

We need to be able to apply our linguistic and theoretical knowledge so that we can enable learning to take place. This requires a wide range of **skills**, many of which are dealt with elsewhere in this book. Examples include: *The skills to transfer our knowledge*

- **interpersonal** skills; the ability to understand our students' needs and meet them, the ability to treat all students equally without showing personal preference, managing groups;

- **organisational** skills; being well prepared, turning up on time, doing the necessary administration properly;

- **adaptability**; teaching well when the only cassette player is being used by the aerobics teacher, or when we have to change classrooms at 30 seconds notice;

- **creativity**; devising varied but appropriate activities and producing or selecting appropriate materials to meet the needs of our students.

New and improved **resources** are continually being produced for language teaching, and yet a surprisingly large number of teachers continue to use books and materials which were originally produced as long ago as the 1950s[2]! While new is, of course, not necessarily better, teachers are sometimes guilty of using material they know and not making the extra effort involved in finding out what else is available and trying something new. *Resources and technology*

Recent developments in **technology** have given teachers the opportunity to improve considerably the quality of the service they provide for their students. Some teachers of adults maintain that the new technology is not available to them, but with a little persistence many are able to obtain at least some of the resources available for the education service as a whole in their area. Technical advice on how to use the equipment is also almost always obtainable, again with a little persistence. With word-processors readily available, semi-legible handwritten handouts should be a thing of the past; videos, cassettes, satellite TV, computer-assisted language learning materials and so on can enrich enormously the language learning environment for our students, and teachers have a responsibility to keep up with new developments and to develop the skills necessary to be able to use them.

Adult education does not exist in a vacuum but is one part of a total educational service provided across the country. Our students also, professionally or as parents or merely as citizens, have links with other sectors of education. As teachers it is important for us to be aware not only of trends and developments which have a direct bearing on our teaching, but also of changes within other sectors, of policies within education as a whole. *The context of adult education*

In spite of current preoccupations with acquiring practical expertise, however, our responsibilities extend beyond the practicalities of the *Agents of change* transfer of a specific skill, because we are also educators in a wider sense. As teachers we may be described as **'agents of change'**:

> *we aim to ... help to bring about changes in skills, knowledge, understanding and behaviour.*[3]

Foreign language teaching offers:

> *a rich and powerful resource to modify insular attitudes, parochialism, narrow home values, prejudice and bigotry, authoritarian and traditional thinking.*[4]

Teaching about another culture makes us reflect on our own culture and has significant and important potential for change.

Current provision of training

The key to 'being a professional' lies in teacher training, and the HMI survey of foreign language courses for adults looked at provision of teacher training courses. Having noted that the vast majority of adult education tutors are part-time, the report concluded that while there was considerable variation of provision between the institutions surveyed:

> *Too often ... it seemed that training for part-time teachers is allocated a rather low priority.*[5]

The wide variation of provision occurs not only between different authorities but also from centre to centre. The range in one county alone is from no provision at all to two Saturday morning workshops a term[2]. Some authorities insist on attendance at a training course to teach adults even if the teacher has a PGCE, while others employ as teachers people with no teaching experience, whose only qualification is being a native speaker of the language. Some provide generic training courses for teachers of any subject to adults, while others provide subject-specific training. Some require attendance at courses and some do not; some require training before starting to teach and others offer the option to train while teaching. Some offer meetings from time to time, often to discuss administrative matters such as books required or enrolment procedures, rather than training courses. In many instances the one common feature of the training available is that teachers attend in their own time and are not paid to do so. The huge variation in the quality of the service provided generally reflects these differences.

In view of the fact that professional support is so often lacking, it is not surprising that adult education tutors still complain of feeling isolated. As many teach in community centres and church halls in small communities, lack of contact with colleagues is a major problem. At in-service courses feedback invariably includes the comment that one of the most useful aspects of the course was meeting colleagues and exchanging ideas and experiences. Having attended courses, teachers who may not have felt the need to be trained often feel so positive about the experience that they are happy to give up their time on a future occasion.

How can we become professional?

There are a number of ways in which part-time tutors to whom no training is offered can address the problem. One is to approach their heads of centre/adult education organisers and to make constructive suggestions as to what is required and how it can best be delivered. Ideally this approach should be made by a group of teachers rather than an individual. This would take time to be implemented, however, and there may be no funds available to support such an initiative.

Self-help

Another option is for teachers to set up their own groups. The **NETWORD** network, organised through CILT, suggests ways of setting up a self-help group[6]. As an organisation with contacts nationally and with its own regular free newsletters, it provides an invaluable source of information and a forum for the exchange of information and ideas.

There are a number of external bodies which can provide further support. As a member of the **Association for Language Learning**[7] one is kept informed about conferences and seminars, as well as receiving regular journals. This is one way of keeping up to date with current trends.

Other sources of information and support are:

★ CILT[6] - an excellent information service;
★ The Central Bureau for Educational Visits and Exchanges[8] - may be able to help in providing funds for maintaining linguistic skills;
★ European Community funding via the LINGUA[9] programme.

For those who wish to become professional in the formal sense of being qualified, there are a number of alternatives available, whether we are interested in pre-service, in-service or refresher courses. Many short courses nowadays may be accredited towards a qualification like a certificate of education, and local organisers should have access to the relevant information about what is available in a particular area. Most of the training courses can be followed part-time to fit in with other commitments. Courses available may focus on teaching **adults**, on teaching **languages**, or on a combination of both.

Becoming qualified

If we are to maintain and develop our professional skills it is vital for us to be self-critical and to be prepared to consider constructive criticism from others. A few moments spent after each lesson in **self-evaluation** is time well spent. A list of specific questions prepared beforehand will help to make the exercise more valuable. The following is a suggested basic list, but it is by no means exhaustive and teachers would no doubt like to develop their own, or use different lists and look at different aspects of lessons at different times[10].

Self-evaluation and appraisal

SELF-EVALUATION QUESTIONS

1. Did I achieve my aims and objectives? If not, what did I not achieve and why not?

2. Which was the most successful part of the lesson, and why? Which was the least successful part of the lesson, and why?

3. Did all the students participate, and if not why not? Did I cater for the mixed ability/levels etc in the group satisfactorily; if not, how could I improve?

4. How would I teach the lesson differently on another occasion?

Many teachers in all sectors of education are uneasy or hostile at the prospect of being **appraised**. The term appraisal is used to refer to formal evaluation by a senior manager; it may consist of the scrutiny of schemes of work, lesson observation, and usually includes an interview with the teacher to discuss the appraiser's observations. If properly constructed, appraisal can be an opportunity for constructive two-way discussion and feedback, at which the teacher as well as the manager can put forward points of view and ideas. Furthermore, if we wish to be taken seriously as professionals, we must be prepared to allow our managers to see what we are doing in our classrooms.

The responsibilities of management

So far in this unit a considerable burden of effort and responsibility has been placed upon the adult education teacher. The dedication and commitment of a teacher, who may be teaching for only four hours a week, with no guarantee of continued employment beyond next week, no sick pay and no holiday pay, cannot be expected to continue ad infinitum. Goodwill eventually runs out, and one of the reasons for the high turnover of adult education teachers - particularly the effective ones - is that they find better conditions of service elsewhere. In order to be professional, teachers need to be treated as professionals. They need to have appropriate support from their managers.

Management is responsible for the framework of the service as a whole:

★ for effective marketing and enrolment,
★ for the provision of a coherent structure and line of progression for students who wish to progress through different levels,
★ for co-ordination and co-operation with neighbouring institutions,
★ for adequate resourcing,
★ for maintaining regular contact with the teachers.

In return managers are entitled to require their teachers to undertake certain professional duties:

★ to attend meetings and training courses;
★ to counsel students;
★ to produce schemes of work.

The **quality** of the service thus provided will be much less hit-and-miss for the students, according to where they happen to live. We would be entering into a '**professional contract**' between the teacher, management and the students, which would give greater satisfaction to all.

The cost involved in the provision of a service of this kind is modest and the potential educational benefits are considerable: if we can fulfil all of the conditions outlined above, we will have the satisfaction of a job well done, and will be in a far stronger position to fight for the maintenance of a valuable service.

References

1. Bates, A W, *Towards a better research framework for evaluating the effectiveness of educational media*, IET paper on broadcasting, Open University (1982).

2. Ainslie, S, *Foreign language courses for adults - the Lancashire survey,* Hugh Baird College, Bootle (1990).

3. Rogers, A, *Teaching adults*, Open University (1986), p 118.

4. Arthur, L, 'Just grist to the mill of Moloch?', *Netword News No. 6, (*1989).

5. DES, *A survey of foreign language courses for adult students in 34 institutions*, a report by HMI, DES (1988).

6. CILT, Regent's College, Inner Circle, Regent's Park, London NW1 4NS.

7. ALL, 16 Regent Place, Rugby CV21 2PN.

8. The Central Bureau for Educational Visits and Exchanges, Seymour Mews House, Seymour Mews, London W1H 9PE; 3 Bruntsfield Crescent, Edinburgh EH10 4HD; 16 Malone Road, Belfast BT9 5BN.

9. UK Lingua Unit, Seymour Mews House, Seymour Mews, London W1H 9PE.

10. Doff, A, *Teach English: a training course for teachers*, CUP (1988), has many examples of self-evaluation sheets, as well as practical ideas for teacher training courses.

Over to you

A.   *A practical
self-help suggestion*

Observing someone else teaching and being observed oneself are both potentially extremely valuable ways of improving one's teaching. They are also extremely easy to set up and cost nothing apart from time. Unfortunately most of us do not like being observed! And done in the wrong way it can be very destructive. The following simple self-help strategy should, however, prevent this from happening:

1) with a colleague/colleagues agree on a list of criteria which you think make up 'good' teaching;

2) ask a colleague to observe you, referring to your agreed list;

3) discuss the lesson afterwards, and maybe revise/add to your list; discuss how you would teach the lesson differently if you did it again;

4) arrange to observe your colleague in the same way.

Your students may like to become involved as well! You may want to produce different lists to look at different aspects of teaching on different occasions. For example, one week you may want to look at patterns of interaction; another week you may want to look at how the different stages of the lesson are introduced. The important thing is that everybody involved has agreed to be so, that everyone knows what the criteria are, and that the agreed objective is to improve performance and not to criticise for the sake of it.

If facilities permit, being videod is usually very salutary but very useful!

A model for your area 1) Look at the criteria selected by teachers in Lancashire as desirable components of effective provision of foreign languages to adults.

a) Staff development - careful recruitment, induction training, schemes of work;
b) Effective marketing and enrolment;
c) Clear course titles and descriptions of course aims and content;
d) Coherent structuring of courses;
e) Accreditation;
f) Better resourcing;
g) Access to and dissemination of information;
h) Flexibility, e.g. in mode of delivery and responsiveness to student need;
i) Agreement between institutions on e.g. vocational/non-vocational distinction; provision of more advanced classes; class size.

2) Do you agree with them? What is missing?

3) Which of the criteria are already met in your area?

4) What practical suggestions would you make to your authority as to ways in which the service in your area could be improved?

5) Which of the criteria are you and your colleagues able to meet yourselves?

5   A suggested approach

The first lesson for beginners: a suggested approach

Stella Hurd

This unit outlines issues which the teacher of a beginners' class will need to address, gives ideas for general and specific preparation and suggestions for obtaining and using information. It is set out in checklist style to facilitate easy access.

Two sample lessons are proposed at the end to provide a basis from which the teacher can work in structuring his or her lesson. They are in no way intended as a prescribed lesson one of a beginners' course. Indeed, if in the process of evaluating the models new ideas emerge to supplement or supplant those suggested, they will have well served their purpose.

Preliminary considerations

Having accepted the post of tutor to a language class of beginners, you will now be turning your attention to the demands about to be made on you and the best way to organise your preparation. You may teach or have taught children or teenagers, but not adults. You may have taught adults but not at beginners' level. You may even have some experience in this field but welcome the opportunity to examine the issues more closely. The many facts about adult learners outlined and examined in units 1-3 need to be assimilated and evaluated in terms of their implications for the way in which you intend to establish teaching and learning styles within your own group of learners. To summarise briefly:

★ Most adults pay to attend and expect value for money.

★ Adult classes are mixed. Students will expect you to respond to their individual learning needs.

★ Adult learners are generally highly motivated, co-operative and responsive. Nevertheless, student drop-out can be high, particularly at basic levels. It is unwise to take that initial motivation for granted. Low numbers mean class closures.

What can the teacher do prior to the class starting?

- ask to sit in on other classes;
- read up on language learning theories (if there is plenty of time) and their practical application;
- study the coursebook thoroughly, along with any accompanying audio and/or video materials;
- find out what equipment is available and what materials exist for language teachers;
- consult other teachers of your language;
- check on the room you have been allocated: access to power points, proximity to other classrooms, presence or absence of curtains/blinds to block out the light, state of blackboard (bear in mind that last-minute room changes are fairly common);
- if you are untrained, find out about training opportunities;
- avail yourself of any opportunities to meet potential students by offering to help at Information, Advice and Guidance Days, Open Days and particularly at Enrolment;
- use every opportunity to keep your own linguistic skills and cultural background knowledge updated.

How should preparation be organised?

Start from the moment of appointment. In adult education it must be remembered that there are no guarantees. If insufficient numbers enrol the course will be cancelled, which will always be a cruel blow to those who are conscientious and keen. On the more positive side, it should be said that preparation is rarely wasted.

Having studied the coursebook and accompanying materials, the next stage is to write a **scheme of work** (see unit 14) for the course, for submission to your Tutor-in-charge or Head of Languages. Seek advice on how to do this. You will find in some centres that it is a collaborative enterprise with all members of the language department taking part, in order to ensure uniformity of format. Other centres may issue a pro-forma for all courses. The scheme of work will give a broad outline of the course with elaboration on teaching methods, aims and anticipated outcomes. It may also include information on target audience and evaluative mechanisms. Preparation will take the form of a detailed **lesson plan** (see unit 8).

What should the first lesson contain?

Like all lessons, a balance of material and activities with clear objectives. Ideally, these should be linguistic but there is a strong case for placing more importance on psychological considerations at this crucial early stage (see unit 1). The teacher's role in the first lesson is primarily to encourage, motivate and support. Learners will gain confidence through an early sense of achievement, however small. It is thus important for them to be able to demonstrate that they have learned something in the first lesson.

A certain part of the first lesson will inevitably be taken up with administrative tasks such as distribution of books, entering names on a register, collecting money, enrolling latecomers and many more. It is all too easy to let these tasks overrun and waste precious time, particularly if you are nervous. Remember that the majority of students will be just as nervous as you, and if a temporary confidence booster is needed, remind yourself that you **do** know more than they do about what they have come to learn, and that their expectations of you will not be clearly formed at this stage. Thorough preparation is your greatest ally and will give you a clear course of action.

What does the teacher need to know about the students?

★ their needs, motivations and aspirations;
★ previous learning experience and knowledge, if any, of the language;
★ desire, if any, for assessment and what kind: flexible? end of year? accreditation towards a degree?
★ mix of characteristics e.g. introvert/extrovert, confident/nervous, fast/slow learner, aggressive/passive;
★ how to help students learn.

How can this information be obtained?

● By means of a simple survey involving questions on reason for enrolling, previous learning, etc. It is best to organise this in terms of a tick-off list of alternatives with a section left for 'other' (see page 143). It must also be borne in mind that a number of students genuinely find it difficult to give a reason for enrolling and may tick anything rather than 'stand out'.

● Through pre-course assessment tests: this may help to reveal 'false beginners'.

● In general class chats: it is important to develop an empathy with the students as early as possible.

● In small group discussions with collective feedback.

● Through close but unobtrusive observation, in the early weeks, of specific factors.

● By developing the ability to 'read between the lines'. This is something akin to imagining the class as a choir with many melodies blending together. It is useful to develop the art of listening to one voice while being aware of the chorus.

What is the value of this information?

In general the teacher will find he or she is:

★ more aware of a variety of needs;
★ less likely to be taken by surprise;

★ in a better position to be flexible;
★ able to anticipate and predict more effectively;

and thus will find it easier to:

★ devise activities more precisely geared to learners' needs;
★ effect modification of course design to fit in with assessment deadlines;
★ plan to give extra help where needed;
★ better organise pairings and groupings.

Such strategies lead to a greater feeling of security among learners and an immediate clarification of the situation for those who are not sure if they have enrolled at the right level. The necessary moves can be made immediately, and there is likely to be less disruption and time-wasting in the following weeks.

There will naturally be a continuing process of observation, monitoring and evaluation, including self-evaluation, which will reveal other important pieces of information as the course unfolds. It is not sufficient to rely entirely upon this method as the only source of feedback in evaluating course effectiveness and student satisfaction. A great deal can be done, as we have seen, to avoid possible pitfalls even before the course starts.

What does the adult learner need to know?

★ details of course and teacher's expectations;
★ language study skills: how to get the most out of the course through adopting good learning habits, setting aside regular time for home study, compiling and filing materials;
★ how to set priorities and achievable objectives;
★ how to record progress and identify gaps in learning;
★ how to interrelate with other course members;
★ how to become independent and take responsibility for one's own learning.

Much of this information could be published in a student's handbook available at enrolment or before. Time devoted to 'learning to learn' is invaluable and will considerably minimise early difficulties in the learning process. It is particularly important for students attending a once-weekly class who need continuity in their learning and advice on how to retain what they have learned.

Additional considerations

● Target language or mother tongue? This is largely a matter of common sense. Conducting all transactions in the **target language** is a laudable aim and should be achieved as early as possible. There will, however, be many stages on the road to success. It is entirely inappropriate to insist on using the target language all the time in the first lesson of a beginners' course. This should be a stimulating, confidence-boosting experience which should leave students optimistic about their own potential and convinced of their ability to learn the language. In the first lesson any target language that is used should be very easy to understand, reinforced heavily with visual clues, props and gestures, and steps should be taken to ensure that there has been complete comprehension. Contact with the target language should be stimulating and not frustrating. This is particularly important in the first lesson where nervousness is probably the overriding emotion. It is equally important that there is a variety of opportunities from lesson one to hear and speak the foreign language and that students are sensitised to the particular sounds of the language they are about to learn.

A delicate balance will need to be achieved in follow-up lessons between ensuring complete comprehension and stretching forward into language that is new. These risks are not for the first lesson.

● Ensure as far as possible a **balance** of language skills from the earliest stages. Most students find listening particularly difficult. If listening material is introduced regularly from lesson one onwards, this skill will develop naturally along with the skills of reading, speaking and writing, and will become an integral part of every lesson.

● Pay particular attention to the establishment of **group dynamics**. This is of crucial importance in the first lesson. You will be faced with a collection of individuals, most of whom will not know anyone else. It is your task to find ways of enabling them to become a group.

● **Keep your promises**. Make a note of all you have promised to do, bring, find out for next week. Keeping a diary can be very helpful. Note down also any feedback you wish to act upon in future lesson planning.

To sum up   **DO**
● be alert for any signs of feedback;
● make a special effort to remember names;
● ensure that everyone has said something in the foreign language by the end of the lesson;
● end the lesson on a high note, even if this entails re-arrangement or omission of material. Ensure that you have whetted the students' appetites and left them wanting more.

   DON'T
● put anyone on the spot;
● be disheartened if you don't get through all the material you have prepared;
● start anything new in the latter stages of the lesson;
● expect too much of yourself or the students.

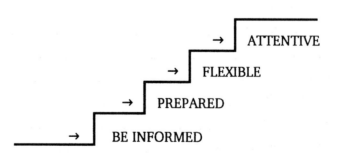

**Sample questionnaire
including brief assessment test (for French)**

(The last section is designed to identify *'faux débutants'* who have enrolled in a beginners class.)

Name:_____

Any course taken in French at or since school:_____
_____

When and where?_____
_____

Why have you enrolled on this course? (Please tick as appropriate)

☐ for business reasons

☐ to gain a qualification

☐ to improve work prospects

☐ because you have visited or intend to visit France

☐ simple interest in learning a foreign language

☐ for family reasons

☐ for social reasons i.e. to meet people

☐ other (please specify if possible)

Fill in the missing words in nos. 1-7. Answer questions 8-10 (It is expected that you will leave this section blank).

1. *Je m'appelle*_____

2. *J'habite*_____

3. *Le jour après dimanche est*_____

4. *Janvier est le premier*_____

5. *Le soir je mange à*_____

6. *Pendant mon temps libre j'aime*_____

7. *Cet été je suis allé(e)*_____

8. *Quelle heure est-il?*_____

9. *Quelle est la date aujourd'hui?*_____

10. *De quelle couleur est votre chemise/jupe/robe/pullover?*_____

_____

Two sample lessons

For a two-hour class, a maximum of fifteen to twenty minutes should suffice for general administration and an introduction to the course. The sample lessons which follow attempt to incorporate short, purposeful linguistic activities with opportunities for students to get to know one another and establish a good group dynamic.

French (Stella Hurd)	**Aims**:

★ to establish a group dynamic through the achievement of brief, simple communicative tasks;

★ to sensitise students to the sounds of the language and its intonation patterns.

Objectives:

★ to demonstrate competence in understanding and giving personal information - name, job, marital status, children - based on listening and reading material;

★ to use with confidence the question: *Comment vous appelez-vous?* and the answer: *Je m'appelle* in pair and group activities.

20 mins
General introduction

● Administration, introduction to the course, brief questionnaire.

15 mins
Introduction to
French pronunciation

● **List** words from the foreign language that are similar, if not identical to English. For French: most sports, television, radio, cinema, and some oddities like 'shampooing' and 'parking'.
Pronounce them individually to demonstrate the difference in the spoken form.
Ask students to **repeat** after you and then say them alternating with a partner. Suggest they imagine (for French) that they are Inspector Clouseau, Maurice Chevalier or Marcel from 'Allo Allo'. You may find it appropriate to introduce gender at this stage.

15 mins
Introduction to
listening skills

● **Play** short extracts containing four or five different foreign languages and ask students to identify which one is the target language.
Introduce yourself in the foreign language with a few props and mimes and ask students to relate back to you what you said. They can invariably do this, much to their surprise.

10 mins
Listening activities

● Some **listening** material: greetings, very simple personal information (two or three short dialogues) with perhaps a grid to complete or specific items to tick or some true/false statements. Nothing too elaborate.

20 mins
Listening and
pronouncing

● Circulate the text of the dialogues and re-play with pauses in which they **read** aloud the missing word. This could be repeated without the text if you feel it is appropriate.

check on meanings   **act out**

Students may well want to know vocabulary to enable them to talk about themselves, e.g. piano tuner or maintenance engineer. It is wise to discourage this as it will involve too much specialist vocabulary and structure for this early stage of learning. Reassure them in a lighthearted way that tonight they can only be Pierre or Chantal, married or single, have one or two children and be a civil servant or a technician.

Take one question and answer only from the dialogue: **Comment vous appelez-vous? Je m'appelle...** this can be practised for real in pairs and groups and is an ideal opportunity for students to work together and get to known each other.

5 mins
Asking and giving
your name

Distribute cards with the name of one half of a famous couple or duo, e.g. Laurel and Hardy, Romeo and Juliet, Napoléon and Joséphine, Hale and Pace. If there are odd numbers in the class, you will have to decide whether to take part or give two students the same name. Students circulate asking **Comment vous appelez-vous?** and answering **Je m'appelle...** until they find their 'other half'.

15 mins
Group activity:
find your partner

Recap of main points. A light activity such as a song, puzzle, poem, joke or cartoon.

10 mins
Recap and
ending activity

Homework.

This lesson leaves 10 minutes for a break or just the flexibility to spend extra time on activities where needed.

Objectives:
★ to provide opportunities for students to get to know each other;
★ to introduce students to the characteristics of the Japanese language: sounds and writing system;
★ to provide students with the language for simple greetings and introductions.

Japanese (Haruko Lewis)

● welcome to each class member on arrival;
● outline of course details: aims and objectives;
course book and related material;
guidelines for learning.

15 mins
General introduction

● some grammatical points;
● vocabulary: demonstration of Japanese words which originated in English. Other examples for students to guess, e.g. TEREBI (television), RAJIO (radio), WAAPURO (word processor), etc;
● pronunciation: students listen to short Japanese words on tape and repeat;
● writing system: brief explanation with some examples on OHP.

30 mins
Introduction to the
Japanese language

● ice-breaker: student 1 gives first name and reason for wanting to learn Japanese. Student 2 repeats the information given by student 1 in the third person: s/he is called ... etc. Student 3 repeats the information given by students 1 and 2, and so on until the last student repeats the information given by everyone. No writing allowed!

25 mins
Meeting and greeting

- teach Japanese for *Please repeat after me*;
- demonstration of words/phrases for greeting:
  e.g. OHAYOO (good morning)
  KONNICHIWA (good afternoon)
  KONBANWA (good evening)
  Students repeat;
- practice activity: students shown two pictures:
  1. representing morning, afternoon or evening;
  2. showing two people bowing to one another.
  Students use correct greeting language according to the time of day shown. Pair work practice to further consolidate the language for greeting.

15 mins
Introducing yourself

- phrases written on BB or OHP:
  KONBANWA (good evening)
  HAJIMEMASHITE (how do you do)
  (WATASHI WA)...DESU (I am)
  DOOZO YOROSHIKU (pleased to meet you)
- demonstration of introductions;
- students introduce themselves using above phrases;
- pair work or small group practice for further consolidation.

15 mins
Mixing activity

- find your partner: each student is given a card with the first name of a famous pair. Pretending to be that person, students circulate introducing themselves to each other until they find their partner. Possible examples: Elizabeth/Philip, Adam/Eve.

This is an extended version of the French group activity, designed to practise all the language introduced in the previous two sections.

10 mins

Recap and homework.

(10 minutes allowed for break or extra time)

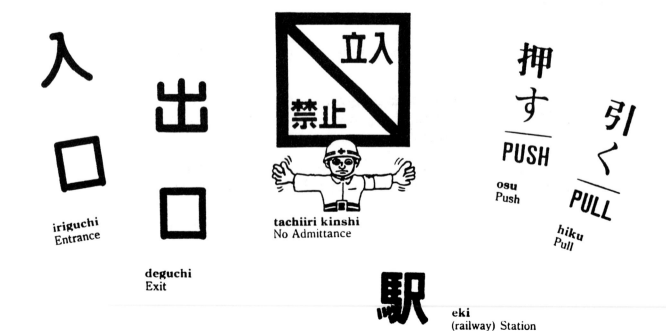

iriguchi
Entrance

deguchi
Exit

tachiiri kinshi
No Admittance

osu
Push

hiku
Pull

eki
(railway) Station

Suggestions for classroom activities

Stella Hurd

There are many activities that can work towards achieving communicative competence, which are relatively simple to set up (a prime consideration) and effective in their outcomes. They have at their core a specific language structure or function to be practised, or body of vocabulary based around a theme to be used in oral exchanges, but are not necessarily confined to just that. A degree of open-endedness is always desirable in order to break as far as possible the relative artificiality of the situation and encourage the maximum personal involvement. It should be added that there are times when activities with no specific linguistic aim will be introduced, purely to promote good group dynamics.

Some key factors to bear in mind are:

★ **accessibility**:
   relating to students' own experience and at an appropriate level

★ **involvement**:
   intrinsically interesting

★ **repetition**:
   needing to get one piece of information from many sources or a lot of information from one source

★ **flexibility**:
   should be possible to use at different levels and to practise different language items

★ **relevance to an integrated skills approach**:
   should be able to be exploited as part of a chain of integrated activities, using different language skills.

The following activities respond to a range of linguistic and functional aims. Those that are particularly suitable for encouraging learners to mix within a group are marked *.

*1

Transparency overlay

General/functional aim: ★ to practise ordering basic items in a *café*, and building up more precise details such as flavours/ingredients and prices.

Linguistic aim: ★ to use with confidence constructions introduced by *à* in the description of flavours/ingredients and prices.

Preparation, method and presentation

Transparencies provide a very flexible and effective teaching aid which can be easily stored and repeatedly used. This is a simple overlay with French examples. It could easily be adapted for other languages as it relies heavily on pictures:

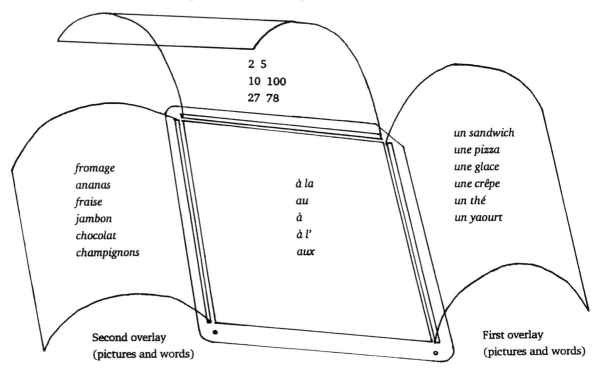

Third overlay
(pictures of coins/notes)

2 5
10 100
27 78

un sandwich
une pizza
une glace
une crêpe
un thé
un yaourt

fromage
ananas
fraise
jambon
chocolat
champignons

à la
au
à
à l'
aux

Second overlay
(pictures and words)

First overlay
(pictures and words)

Procedure:

Stage 1:   identify the items
Stage 2:   overlay the flavours/ingredients: build up sentences
Stage 3:   overlay the prices: build up more information and longer sentences

The activity can be greatly enlivened by moving the second and third overlays up and down to produced amusing combinations: e.g. *Une glace aux champignons à 100F* (a mushroom ice cream for 100F!).

Follow-up could take the form of a situation in a *café*, either working as a whole group with teacher as waiter, or in small groups or pairs. Students could then be invited to make up other combinations based on what they have already learned.

Other examples of overlay use are to be found in Duncan Sidwell's *Modern language learning*. His pair work series in French *Toi et moi* and German *Du und Ich* can also be easily adapted for the overhead projector.

General/functional aim ★ to provide opportunities to move from pre-communicative linguistic forms to communicative language functions. To strengthen listening skills.

Linguistic aim ★ flexible. Here, to practise the past (perfect) tense in questions and affirmative and negative statements.

2
Creative use of 'controlled' dialogues

Preparation, method and presentation

A recording is prepared or selected which is suitable for identification and practice of a particular linguistic form: e.g. a tense, part of speech, vocabulary relating to a particular area of use. The key words are blanked out.

Preliminary task

to complete the missing words in the text, in this case examples of the perfect tense.

Procedure:

● working in pairs, students together make an 'educated guess' on what the missing words might be. These might be presented at the bottom of the text, jumbled up, or not present at all.

● the recording is played three times:

1. without pauses, for general gist;
2. with several pauses to enable students to identify and write in the missing words, after which, working in pairs, they compare their work so far;
3. with a pause after each blank, for verification purposes.

● students make a final check with the original, displayed preferably on the OHP, with the missing words highlighted for repetition.

Development:

● students act out dialogue in pairs;
● each student is then given a new version of their role in which certain elements have been changed;

- students act out again and attempt to spot the changes in their partner's script through listening carefully, e.g.:

A   What did you do last Sunday?
B   Sunday? No, Saturday! I went to see Claire.
A   Claire? No, you went to see Sarah! And what did you do?
B   We went to the park.
A   The park? You didn't go to the swimming pool? etc.

Alternatively, sentences can remain unfinished and students provide their own version, e.g.:

A   What did you do last...?
B   I...
A   What time did you...?
B   About...

Further development for more advanced learners can encourage a sharp move along the controlled ↔ free continuum. Students are given cards simply outlining a role they are to play, e.g.:

Role A: You are an anxious parent confronting your teenage son/daughter who has just rolled in late. Start the conversation.

Role B: You are a 16-year-old boy/girl who should have been home by midnight. It is now 2 a.m. One of your parents opens the door and confronts you. Explain what happened as plausibly as possible.

---

*3

Split sentences, dialogues, questions, answers

General/functional aim   ★ to focus on specific language structures and patterns; to encourage students to develop good listening and speaking skills.

Linguistic aim   ★ flexible. Here, to practice:

- example (i): 'if' clauses in French with imperfect and conditional tenses
- example (ii): a range of simple language items that might occur in a typical 'asking the way' exchange, e.g. (in French) *pour aller à, à pied, à gauche, c'est ça, je vous en prie*

Preparation, method and presentation

Split sentences: Each students is given a **card** on which is written the first or second half of a sentence. Students must find the missing half of their sentence. They do this by circulating, stopping frequently to **say** to another student what is on their card and **listen** to what is on his/her card. At no time may they look at another card. If students think they 'match', they make a note of the whole sentence and continue to circulate and talk to others to see how many other sentences are possible. It is important at the preparation stage to make several link-ups possible:

- to prolong the game until everyone has 'found' their missing half;
- to increase opportunities for language manipulation within a given form.

This activity is very useful for:

- practising a specific linguistic form or language for a specific function;
- diagnosing learners' problems;
- encouraging students to relax and have fun.

The 'fun' element is intensified if a few grammatically acceptable, yet amusing or nonsensical possible sentence combinations are included. Communication under these circumstances is unlikely to be very meaningful!

Example (i):
To practise the use of tenses in sentences containing 'if' clauses in French:

A [first half of sentence]	B (second half)
Si j'avais 100 000 FF [If I had 100 000FF]	*j'aurais mal à la gorge* (I would have a sore throat)
Si j'étais sale [If I was dirty]	*je serais ravi(e)* (I would be delighted)
Si je chantais tout le temps [If I sang all the time]	*je prendrais une douche* (I would have a shower)
Si j'avais faim [If I was hungry]	*j'appellerais un mécanicien* (I would call a mechanic)
Si ma voiture tombait en panne [If my car broke down]	*je mangerais un sandwich* (I would eat a sandwich)

... and so on.

The same procedure is adopted to practise matching questions and answers. Students are often willing to extend into a spontaneous conversation any ideas that the original question/answer may spark off. They are thus in a position to move closer towards autonomous language use and to identify what other language they need to know at this point.

Example (ii):
To match up sentence halves and arrange them into a dialogue. The oblique in the example that follows marks where the sentence could be split for the first stage of the activity. This particular example would be suitable for a class of sixteen students. The dialogue is of the type to be found in most coursebooks for beginners:

Pardon/madame
(Excuse me)
Pour aller à / la gare s'il vous plaît?
(How do I get to the station please?)
Vous êtes / à pied?
(Are you walking?)
Oui / c'est ça
(Yes, that's right)
Alors, vous tournez / à gauche aux feux rouges
(Well, you turn left at the traffic lights)
Et c'est à 200 metres / sur votre droite
(And it's 200 metres away on your right)
Je vous / remercie beaucoup, Madame
(Thank you very much)
Je vous / en prie
(Don't mention it)

Stage 1:   distribution of cards, and matching up to form sentences

Stage 2:   working in pairs representing the two halves of the sentence, students circulate once more and arrange themselves in the order of the dialogue in a circle

Stage 3:   teacher works through dialogue with students, making any necessary re-arrangements to the circle

Stage 4:   final re-reading. By this time it may be appropriate to act out the dialogue from memory to make it less artificial and enable students to feel themselves into the role in a more realistic way.

---

*4 **Information gap**	***General/functional aim***	★ to give and receive information necessary for the completion of a task.
	Linguistic aim	★ flexible, dependent on topic selected.

Examples for working in pairs, small groups and large groups follow:

Working in pairs

Who else lives in your block of flats?

You and your partner both have some information which the other needs in order to stockpile a full list of occupants and some personal details about them:

A	B
Mr Bloggs, widower, four cats	Mrs James, divorced, two children
Mrs Dukes, tall, brown hair lives on fourth floor	Ms Dunn, comes from London, leaves at 7.30 every morning

This could be varied by providing each student with some details of each occupant but omitting the same kind of information each time in order to encourage the asking of specific questions.

An obvious follow-up would be a collective reporting back of the pooled information.

The way in which the task is presented is an important consideration. Why is this information needed: Are you investigating a crime? Are you young people who have just moved in and are wanting to make new friends? What will you do with it afterwards?

A useful resource book for this type of pair work exercise, available in more than one language, is the Macmillan series *Take your partners* (see unit 13: Further reading on communicative activities).

Train information for Pratton → Stewbury

Working in small groups

A simple task for basic level groups. Working in fours, each student is given two items of information relating to train services, and two questions to formulate, e.g.

A	C
Dep. morning 9.56 a.m.	Arr. afternoon 4.59 p.m.
Single: £27.48	Return: £45.50
Dep. afternoon ?	Dep. morning ?
Platform ?	Arr. morning ?

B	D
Platform 8 (both trains)	Arr. morning 11.32 a.m.
Buffet facilities (both trains)	Dep. afternoon 3.21 p.m.
Arr. afternoon ?	Single ticket ?
Return ticket ?	Buffet facilities ?

Similar types of activities can be found in a number of resource books for language teachers, of particular note: *Developing communication skills* (see unit 13: Further reading on communicative activities).

The principle for this type of activity is the same as that underlying small group work, in that information must be obtained from more than one source and be imparted to more than one person. It is a useful method to adopt to get a class to 'gel', to encourage all members of the group to work co-operatively and with a common goal. Whole group activities that have been shown to work particularly well at different levels and can be easily modified to fit the needs of a particular group can be found in a variety of resource books, of which the following are a small representation (see unit 13: References and further reading on communicative activities):

Working as a whole group

From Harrap's *Communication Games*:
'Nosey Neighbours':
>By pooling their information the group must attempt to find out what is going on at house no. 5

'Robert's Busy Day':
>Each student must complete Robert's diary by putting questions to the other group members.

From CUP's *Keep Talking*:
'Baker Street':
> Each student receives a piece of paper with some information on it about an occupant of Baker Street. The students share their information and use it to complete a grid representing the street.

See also *Communicative language teaching* (Littlewood, W; CUP, 1981) for more ideas.

This kind of activity in which information is shared among a whole group or in small groups works well in a number of situations: whodunnit?, ideal partners, finding the best route, etc. A successful classroom experience is usually all it takes for an enthusiastic teacher to develop new ideas and variations on a theme.

---

5 **Information exchange (advanced level)**	***General/functional aim***	★ to convey accurately the main details of a story or event by working in pairs and/or small groups.
	Linguistic aim	★ flexible, dependent upon text(s) selected. Activity useful for general practice of language needed for 'coping', e.g. 'could you repeat that', 'I didn't quite get that', 'did you say that ...?', etc.

Preparation, method and presentation

Students work in pairs and are given a short story or newspaper article to discuss and summarise orally (different stories for each pair). They note down the main points in the target language and practise relating them to their partner.

After a given time limit, new pairs are formed and the stories exchanged with no notes being taken.

Students continue to form new pairs when the teacher says 'All change' and relate the story *they have just heard* to the new partner. After three or four changes, students return to their places and some are selected to relate the story they have just heard. All those who have heard it already are at liberty to 'chip in' if the teller flounders or gets the details wrong. This is really a more elaborate version of 'Chinese Whispers'. It is useful for demonstrating the need for clear and effective speaking skills, for testing listening skills, for highlighting language gaps and for encouraging the development of good coping strategies when comprehension is limited.

Another version of information exchange which works well with longer newspaper articles or literary extracts incorporates the task of 'jigsaw' reading. As before, students work in pairs, this time on a section of the text. They then form groups, with each member representing one section, and together re-construct the text, using only the target language. The logistics of this type of activity can be daunting and it needs thorough planning. For a group of twelve students, the text would ideally be divided into six sections:

Stage 1:   six pairs each working on a different section;
Stage 2:   two groups of six each representing a different section and
           together making up the entire text.

The major practical problem is not knowing in advance how many students
are going to be present. It is worth having more than one text available,
suitable for different combinations and numbers of students.
Another possibility is to appoint one student for each group as
spokesperson. He or she will have had access to the whole text during the
preparation pair work stage, but not long enough to thoroughly absorb all
its contents. It is his or her task to give a final *resumé* from the individual
contributions.

The next three activities require little or no preparation and are designed
for a class of adult students working together towards the same end, either
as one whole group throughout, or at different stages splitting into smaller
groups or pairs. The objective in each case is accurate oral production of
the verb endings in a particular tense or mood.

		6
General/functional aim	★ to practise verb endings in a chosen tense both receptively and productively.	**Memory test**
Linguistic aim	★ flexible. Here, to practise verb endings in a given tense.	

Preparation, method and presentation

The teacher prepares ten sentences, using one tense throughout to
describe, for example, in French 'what happened yesterday' (perfect tense)
or 'childhood hobbies' (imperfect tense), 'an ideal Sunday' (conditional
tense), or 'what I had achieved by the age of twenty-one' (pluperfect
tense).

Procedure

The teacher reads out the sentences twice to the class with a very brief
introduction to set the scene, the first time at a slightly slower than
average speaking speed.

Students are then asked, working in pairs, to endeavour to re-construct the
events they have just heard. To do this they are required to use the 'he or
she' form of the verb. The only help they are given is the number of
sentences to remember.

After an agreed time each pair is asked to contribute a sentence, this
time speaking directly to the teacher and therefore using the 'you' form of
the verb.

An activity that is particularly suitable at the start of a class.

7

Guessing game

A combined version of 'What's my line?' and 'Twenty questions'

General/functional aim ★ to develop good receptive and productive skills; to encourage a co-
operative approach to solving a
problem; to have fun!

Linguistic aim ★ to ask appropriate yes/no questions
in a given tense.

Preparation, method and presentation

The teacher prepares one sentence to describe his/her imaginary job,
past, present or future, or perhaps a job s/he would regard as ideal.
Students must guess what the job is by asking questions in the appropriate
tense which can only be answered by yes or no. It is usually the case that
students need some guidance on the kinds of questions they can ask to
gradually elicit more and more helpful information, in order to avoid a
situation in which they simply suggest one job after another, e.g. (past)
'did you work alone?' 'were the hours regular?' 'was it well paid?' 'did you
have to wear a uniform?' etc.

It is a good idea to insist that no-one name a job until a pre-
determined number of questions has been asked. The longer it takes, the
more practice students will have in asking questions using a particular
tense. For this reason it is obviously wise to choose the job very carefully:
ultimately 'guessable' but far from obvious.

*8

Making choices

General/functional aim ★ to conduct a light-hearted survey
through the use of individual, pair
and group work.

Linguistic aim ★ to consolidate verb endings of a
given tense allowing for an element
of choice and unpredictability; to
practise question and answer forms
in the given tense(s).

Preparation, method and presentation

The teacher writes up on the blackboard or OHP the start of a sentence
on the left with a choice of possible endings on the right, with all verbs in
the infinitive, e.g.:

If I were to win the pools   buy a flat on the Cote d'Azur
make a large donation to charity
give up work
have the holiday of a lifetime

each student makes a silent individual choice of what he or she would
do from the list of four alternatives;

- the teacher picks a student and suggests a choice he or she might have made, e.g.: 'If you were to win the pools, would you give up work?' (**you** form of verb);

- student confirms or denies, using whole sentences (**I** form of verb);

- activity passes to students with teacher acting only as observer/monitor.

If the asker guessed correctly he or she scores one point. If not, the student answering states what he or she in fact chose, e.g.:
'No, if I were to win the pools I would buy a flat on the Cote d'Azur.'

...and the game continues until each student has asked and/or answered a question. In a large group it is best to allow one or the other; otherwise the activity can take too long.

Follow-up

Students can score further points for each correct sentence they make stating another student's choice, e.g.:
'If Jean were to win the pools she would have the holiday of a lifetime.'

(**he** or **she** form of verb)

Final stage

Students add up their points and the winner is identified!

The next three activities are slightly more elaborate and some require a certain amount of preparation of materials which can be re-used. They are more open-ended and flexible: less product-oriented and prescriptive.

General/functional aim	★ to ask, answer, suggest, affirm or deny according to individual choice.	**9**
Linguistic aim	★ Primary: to practise question and answer in the perfect tense.	**Making and using grids**
	★ Secondary: to encourage accurate use of prepositions; to practise numbers and dates; to extend vocabulary.	

Preparation, method and presentation

The teacher draws a series of vertical lines on the blackboard to make six columns, giving each an appropriate heading, depending on the nature of the exercise.

This particular example centres round holidays:

NAME   WHERE WENT   WHEN   HOW   WITH WHOM   WHAT DID

- teacher completes grid for person A;
- students suggest material for completing the grid a further three times in response to teacher's questions, e.g. 'What is the second person called?' 'Where did s/he go on holiday?' etc;
- when the grid is complete there are a variety of ways in which it can be exploited, teacher to student or student to student:
  - direct questions;
  - true/false statements;
  - beginnings of sentences to be finished;
  - moving from grid to pair-work discussions on own holidays etc.

---

*10

Pair matching

General/functional aim   ★ to encourage good group dynamics in solving a problem through the exchange of information; to promote and extend receptive and productive skills.

Linguistic aim   ★ to ask questions and make statements using prepositions and pronouns in the perfect tense.

Preparation, method and presentation

This activity requires students to move around the room and is therefore unsuitable for classes taking place in cramped conditions. It could, however, be adapted if necessary.

The teacher prepares one set of cards to represent a group of detectives, and a second set to represent a group of criminals sought after by the detectives. The class is divided into detectives and criminals. Each detective is given a card with details of one criminal's activities; each criminal is given a card with details of his/her activities. The detectives must succeed in 'catching' their criminal, i.e. the one who matches the details on their card, by circulating and asking questions, e.g.:

'Where were you on the night of 15 July?' Criminals are, of course required to be honest on this occasion!

If the teacher wishes to use this activity to focus on the use of pronouns, it is advisable to spend more time than usual demonstrating the relevant language structures to the whole group, through conducting several practice exchanges between teacher and student, and/or pairs of students.

A useful follow-up can be a report in the form of separate statements from each detective or criminal individually (using I or s/he verb forms) or from the paired detective and criminal alternating statements (we verb form).

This activity could also be used to practise reported speech and the relevant changes in tense.

A piece of written work could be suggested for homework, based on information gained from the oral exchanges in class.

As with most language games and activities teachers can adapt and modify the basic idea to suit their own and their students' ends.

General/functional aim	★ to encourage good group dynamics through the exchange of personal information.	***11** **Survey**
Linguistic aim	★ to use reflexive verbs in questions, statements, negatives, present and past tenses.	

Preparation, method and presentation

The teacher and/or students prepare a set of questions designed to find out about the daily routine or lives in general of other members of the class, e.g.:

'What time do you get up in the morning?' 'How do you get to work?' 'Do you have much time for relaxation?' etc.

Students can either pool their questions and collectively decide on the ten most interesting ones for a class survey, keep their own individual set and conduct a 'private' survey within a small group, or work with a partner to compile the final set of questions and then join up with another pair to exchange question and answer. The final decision has, as always, to be based on the needs of a particular group and the practical possibilities for classroom exploitation.

The most important consideration in setting up this activity is that students know what they are doing, that they are all actively engaged and have a goal towards which they are working.

The follow-up could consist of a free exchange of information among students on the results of their survey or surveys. It could be more structured to involve some kind of comparative or statistical result. Alternatively, students could be asked to prepare some statements at home to be handed in at the next lesson. Teacher, having corrected any mistakes, writes up the statements with each word on a separate card and carefully places them in separate envelopes. At a given point in the future students are given an envelope and, working in pairs, attempt to put the cards in the right order to produce the original statement. This can be greatly enlivened by introducing a note of competition, e.g. giving a time limit and seeing how many correct statements can be made within it.

General/functional aim	★ through collective endeavour to build up words relevant to a particular topic.	**12** **Extending** **vocabulary**
Linguistic aim	★ flexible, can be adapted to suit the needs of any group of language learners.	

Preparation, method and presentation

This activity is very useful for introducing a topic and at the same time recapping and extending vocabulary.

The teacher draws a sun on the blackboard or OHP with several rays extending from all over its outer edge. In the middle of the sun the teacher writes in the topic, e.g. Christmas.

Students are invited to contribute any words they can think of connected with the theme of Christmas, e.g. turkey, presents, snow, eat, etc. Teacher writes these words at the end of the rays.

A productive follow-up is the formation of sentences around these words which students can work on in pairs. A more advanced activity would be a story or personal account based around the vocabulary.

The advantage of this kind of activity is the simplicity of preparation and the infinite flexibility it allows for a variety of follow-up activities to suit different levels and purposes, ranging from teacher-controlled and semi-controlled to almost entirely student-controlled.

Some excellent ideas for learning and storing new words are to be found in the *Authentik user's guide* (see unit 12: References). The authors use a range of techniques to help learners remember new words, e.g. creating sets of words with similar meanings, building hierarchies of words within a group, drawing diagrams of overlapping circles to provide for the different sets in which a word might be placed, writing new words on Post-its and physically sticking them into a scrapbook within the correct set or category with the possibility of moving them around as new sets emerge in which they could also find a place.

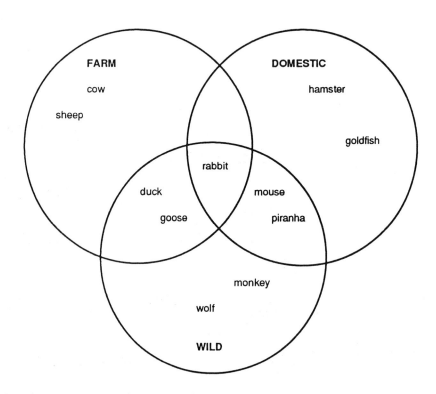

D Little & S Devitt, *Authentik user's guide,*
Authentik Language Learning Resources Ltd, 1991.

Students can also 'brainstorm' their own 'connections' for a given word, to produce a 'word network', or sort words into groups and then find out if another learner can discover what the groups have in common.

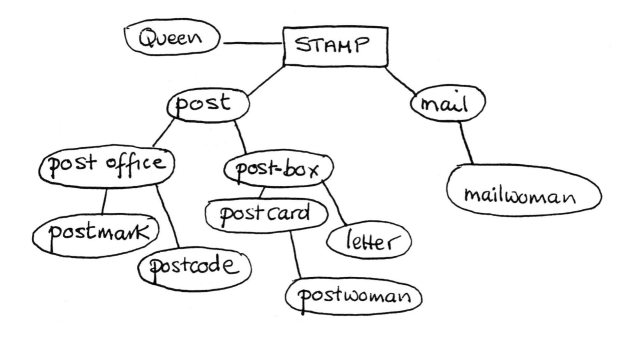

G Ellis & B Sinclair, *Learning to learn English*, CUP, 1989.

About the contributors

Susan Ainslie

After five years of teaching French and German in a secondary school, Susan Ainslie did an MA in Education followed by a year's teaching in Iran. She then undertook a PhD entitled 'Intensive language learning: a multi-media approach', while teaching a range of once-a-week and intensive course to adults and businessmen. She has run many teacher training courses for teachers of adults and co-ordinated the provision of adult language courses in one area. As an advisory teacher in Lancashire she carried out a survey of adult education in that county. She is currently foreign language coordinator at Hugh Baird Tertiary College, Bootle.

Lore Arthur

Lore Arthur is a lecturer in Continuing Education/Languages at Goldsmiths' College, University of London, where she is in charge of a large languages section, teacher training and professional development for teachers in adult, further and higher education. In addition, she lectures and researches at postgraduate level on adult education. She has previously worked for several years as a translator/interpreter and as a part-time language teacher in a variety of adult education institutes as well as in industry and commerce.

Stella Hurd

Stella Hurd was Senior Tutor-in-charge at the College of Adult Education in Wolverhampton before taking up a post as a lecturer in French at the University of Central Lancashire in September 1992. She has wide experience of teaching, training, course design and materials development, and is an active member of the CILT Adult Education working party and the NETWORD editorial group.

Doreen Markam

Doreen Markam's teaching career has taken her into secondary, further and higher education in both England and France. While lecturing at the Université de Paris X (Nanterre) she first became involved in the preparation of independent learning materials for language laboratory and radio, and cassettes for distance learning. For the past six years she has been Senior Course Tutor in foreign languages at Clarendon College of Further Education, Nottingham, and is regional co-ordinator for the Institute of Linguists. The College runs a comprehensive range of courses for full-time and part-time students, as well as providing a language tuition service for local firms.

Alan Moys

In a professional career devoted to the teaching and learning of languages, Alan Moys has been a teacher of both children and adults, a teacher trainer, and a local education authority adviser. From 1978-92 his work took him to CILT, first as Deputy Director, then as Director. He had a central role in the conception and development of CILT's NETWORD initiative. He has written materials for French at various levels, from primary school to adult education.

Duncan Sidwell

Duncan Sidwell is a Leicestershire LEA adviser. He taught in a variety of schools including a Leicestershire community college before becoming an adviser, a post which involves the provision of much in-service education for teachers of languages in all phases of education. He has had a long association with adult education both as a tutor and trainer of tutors, developing training materials as part of this function. He has published a number of articles on aspects of language learning, and books for language learning in German and French.

Rita Sutton

Rita Sutton is Head of German at the Brasshouse Centre, Birmingham, visiting tutor at the Hill Residential College, Abergavenny, and visiting speaker at NETWORD groups in the West Midlands, Avon, Shropshire and Lincolnshire. She has worked with tutors from the Goethe-Institut on teacher training courses and has taught EFL in Britain and in Germany. She is a regular contributor to the Birmingham and Midland, and the Coventry German Clubs.

Useful addresses

ALL (Association for Language Learning)
16 Regent Place
Rugby
CV21 2DN
Tel: 0788 546 443

Associated Examining Board
Stag Hill House
Guildford
Surrey GU2 5XJ
Tel: 0483 300 152

Certificate of further studies: French for business and German for business. One year courses for post-16 and access students.

BBC Educational Services
BBC Broadcasting House
Pebbel Mill Road
Birmingham B5 7QQ
Information Unit in London
Tel: 081 746 1111

CILT (Centre for Information on Language Teaching and Research)
Regent's College
Regent's Park
London NW1 4NS
Tel: 071 486 8221

City and Guilds of London Institute
46 Britannia Street
London WC1X 9RG
TEl: 071 278 2468

Modern language schemes open to candidates of all ages.

Europa Centre
The Walk
Hornchurch
Essex RM11 3TL
Tel: 0708 445 694

Language simulation centre. A French (or German, or Spanish) village can be created to accommodate visits by students - this has been taken up by schools in particular but AE tutors have also taken advantage of the facility.

Contact the Service for details and availability of:
Diplôme Elémentaire de Langue Française (DELF)
and the *Diplôme Approfondi de Langue Française* (DALF).

Offers a number of examinations suitable for adults, including
business language.

Public examinations are available in a wide range of
languages, for both the general and specialist user.

UK address:
IBO Examinations Office
Pascal Close
St Mellons, Cardiff
S Glamorgan CF3 0YP
Tel: 0222 770 770

Language examinations for adults. Languages: Danish, Dutch,
English, French, German, Italian, Japanese, Russian, Spanish.

Leading EFL school which has now diversified into
foreign language teaching.

Specialist college of AE with good reputation for teaching
languages. Offer personalised open/distance learning courses,
backed up with appropriate materials for a number of
languages.

Administer and support the most widely used Graded
Objectives scheme in AE. Provide syllabuses in a
number of European and non-European languages
and are developing support materials for students.

Responsible for developing a system of nationally-defined
levels for language use in employment.

French Embassy
Service Culturel
23 Cromwell Road
London SW7 2EL
Tel: 071 581 5292

Further Education Unit
Citadel Place
Tinworth Street
London SE11 5EH
Tel: 071 962 1280

Goethe-Institut
50 Princes Gate
London SW2 2PH
Tel: 071 581 3344

Institute of Linguists
24a Highbury Grove
London N5 2EA
Tel: 071 359 7445

International Baccalaureate
Office du Baccalaureat
International
Route des Morillons 15
CH-1218 Grand-Saconnex
Geneva, Switzerland
Tel: 022 91 02 74

ICC (International Certificate Conference)
Deutscher Volkshochschul-Verband
Holzhausenstrasse 21
D-6000 Frankfurt, Germany

International House
106 Picadilly
London W1V 9FL

Lancashire College
Southport Road
Chorley, Lancashire PR7 1NB
Tel: 0257 276 719

Languages Development Centre
St Martin's College
Lancaster, LA1 3JD
Tel: 0524 32423

The Languages Lead Body
c/o CILT, see above.

LEXCEL (Language Export Centre)
50-52 Putney Hill
London SW15 6QX
Tel: 081 780 0543

London Chamber of Commerce and Industry Examinations Board
Marlow House
Station Road
Sidcup, Kent DA15 7BJ
Tel: 081 302 4169

Offers a range of practical language assessments and examinations orientated to work.

National Extension College
18 Brooklands Avenue
Cambridge CB2 2HN
Tel: 0223 316 644

Leading correspondence college. Offers language tuition at beginners' and GCSE levels. Also offers tuition for Institute of Linguists exams, and towards the University of London external BA in French, German, Italian and Spanish.

NIACE (National Institute of Adult Continuing Education)
19b De Montfort Street
Leicester LE1 7GE
Tel: 0533 551 451

Among their publications are the journal *Adults Learning* and the series *Adult Learning Strategies and Approaches,* including two modern languages titles.

Pitman Examinations Institute
Catteshall Manor
Godalming
Surrey GU7 1UU
Tel: 0483 415 311

Examinations appropriate for candidates studying at school or college before employment and for those acquiring or updating skills in employment.

Royal Society of Arts Examinations Board
Progress House
Westwood Business Park
Westwood Way
Coventry CV4 8HS
Tel: 0203 470 033

Offers a wide range of language examinations in commercial, business and other fields. All the schemes are designed to equip the individual with a practical knowledge of a language and most are geared to meeting the requirements of an employer.

SCOTVEC (Scottish Vocational Education Council)
Hanover House
24 Douglas Street
Glasgow G2 7NQ
Tel: 041 248 7900

SCOTVEC modules are designed to meet the specific needs of employers in Scotland and to enable holders to progress into higher education courses.

Spanish Chamber of Commerce
5 Cavendish Square
London W1M ODP
Tel: 071 637 9061

Offers an advanced Diploma in Business Spanish.

Spanish Embassy
Education Office
20 Peel Street
London W8 7PD
Tel: 071 727 2462

Offers two diploma examinations for adults.

York University Language Materials Development Unit
King's Manor
York YO1 2EP
Tel: 0904 433 951

LASER Project (Languages at School for Employment and Recreation). For post-16, non-specialist students who already have some knowledge of the language.